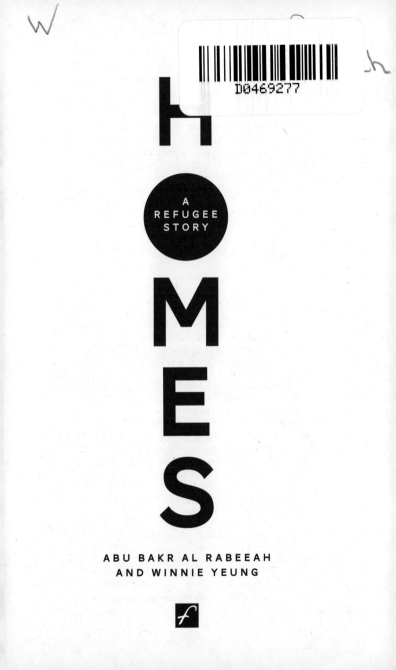

H

O

A
REFUGEE
STORY

M

E

S

ABU BAKR AL RABEEAH
AND WINNIE YEUNG

Published with the generous assistance of the Canada Council for the Arts and the Alberta Media Fund.

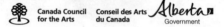

Freehand Books
515 – 815 1st Street SW   Calgary, Alberta   T2P 1N3
www.freehand-books.com

Book orders: LitDistCo
8300 Lawson Road   Milton, Ontario   L9T 0A4
Telephone: 1-800-591-6250   Fax: 1-800-591-6251
orders@litdistco.ca   www.litdistco.ca

Library and Archives Canada Cataloguing in Publication
al Rabeeah, Abu Bakr, 2001–, author
Homes : a refugee story / Abu Bakr al Rabeeah with Winnie Yeung.
Issued in print and electronic formats. ISBN 978-1-988298-28-3 (softcover).
ISBN 978-1-988298-29-0 (epub).   ISBN 978-1-988298-30-6 (pdf)
1. al Rabeeah, Abu Bakr, 2001–. 2. Refugee children — Iraq — Biography.
3. Refugee children — Alberta — Edmonton — Biography. 4. Syria —
History — Civil War, 2011– — Personal narratives, Iraqi. 5. Syria —
History — Civil War, 2011– — Refugees — Alberta — Edmonton —
Biography. I. Yeung, Winnie, 1982–, author II. Title.
HV640.5.I76A47 2018   305.9'06914092   C2018-900161-5   C2018-900162-3

Edited by Barbara Scott
Book design by Natalie Olsen, Kisscut Design
Cover photos © Pat Stornebrink (top) and OBJM (bottom) / Shutterstock
Photo of Abu Bakr al Rabeeah by Samuel Sir
Photo of Winnie Yeung by Heiko Ryll
Printed on recycled paper and bound in Canada

For
Abu Bakr al Rabeeah

"Our childhood is at war with us."

HISHAM AL-JOKH

"Eulogy for Arabism"

Abu Bakr al Rabeeah's family and friends:

(pronounced "Abu ba-CAR al Rah-BEE-ah")

ABU BAKR our protagonist, often called Bakr

HAFEDH AND NIHAD his father and mother

NASER his older brother

MARYAM, ABEER, AIESHA, ASMAA his older sisters

ABRAR AND ALUSH his younger sister and brother

UNCLE MOHAMMED AND AUNT ATEKA Bakr's aunt and uncle

YOUSEF, ABDIL AZIZ, IBRAHIM, DILAL their children, Bakr's cousins

UNCLE NAJIM AND AUNT MUNA Bakr's aunt and uncle

ABDULLAH, HANEEN, ALI, RAIYAN, ISLAM, MARAM their children, Bakr's cousins

GRANDMOTHER MARYAM Bakr's grandmother

AMRO Bakr's best friend

ALI a friend of Bakr and Amro's

Where Did the Sun Go?

Every Friday on the way home from the noon prayer service, *Salat al Jum'ah*, Father stopped to buy fresh fruit from the street vendors. Our mosque was barely a block from our apartment and the walk home was always a loud, lively time, with neighbours and friends catching up at the end of the week. On the day of Father's birthday, April 18, he bought fruit for the family as usual but rather than lingering to chat, he hurried home. All morning, the fighter jets had screamed by.

In the weeks before, every mosque in our neighbourhood, Akrama, had been attacked. Father texted me to go straight home after the service.

I always looked forward to *Salat al Jum'ah.* The comfort of belonging, Father in his white, ankle-length *thawb* tunic, the soothing prayers of peace murmured shoulder to shoulder with friends. I always went with my buddies or cousins, and on this particular afternoon, my neighbour and best friend, Amro, and I laughed as we joined the sea of people spilling out onto the packed street. "The sheikh, he lives in the mosque. *W'Allah!* Trust me, I know," I boasted as we approached our usual meeting spot outside.

"Ugh, no! You think you know everything, Bakr, but bet you he doesn't," insisted Amro.

"*W'Allah!* I swear! Fine, loser buys sodas!"

Our friend Ali sauntered up to us, hand outstretched, and I clasped it firmly. "*Jum'ah mubarak.* Blessed Friday, my friend. Hey, settle this bet fo —"

I was just pulling my hand away from Ali's when the blast hit us. Time expanded and stretched; I saw and felt everything in a disjointed way that seemed too slow to be real. As I fell back, I heard the low *whoooosh* of the taxi full of explosives shooting straight up into the clear blue sky, blocking out the sunlight. In that moment, all I could think was, "Where did the sun go?" The car came crashing down, twice as fast. We were thrown to the ground and showered with gravel and sand. In action movies, the hero always has ringing ears after an explosion and all sound is muffled. That wasn't true for me. The world was muffled for only a split second and then screams filled my ears and Father's voice pierced through the mayhem. "Abu Bakr! Abu Bakr! Abu Bakr!"

That's the sound I still hear when I think about my first car bomb: Father screaming my name.

I dragged myself up and spun towards his shouts.

Father was weaving through the desperate crowds and when he reached me, he grabbed me by the shoulders and turned me this way and that, like a man inspecting a melon at the souk. Satisfied that I was okay, he steered me home.

Moments before, the street in front of our apartment had been filled with people laughing and chatting. Now there was only chaos. Feet running, voices shouting, arms gripping wounds, cellphones frantically trying to document the destruction. The flaming shell of the taxi was only steps from our apartment building. Terrified of what we might find, we rushed through the garden and into our suite. The living room and kitchen were abandoned with lunch half laid-out on the table. Where was everyone?

We heard noises coming from my parents' bedroom. The rest of my family was safe, crammed into the small room. My older brother, Naser, told us that when the bomb exploded, he'd been stretched out on the couch watching TV. Mother and my sister Abeer were cooking in the kitchen. Aiesha and Maryam were in their bedroom, Aiesha texting a friend and Maryam finishing her prayers. Thank God Maryam was kneeling far from the window, which shattered from the force of the explosion. At the sound of the blast, they all took shelter in my parents' bedroom where Asmaa had been with the two youngest, Abrar and Alush, helping them get ready for the day. Alush was jumping around with a cotton swab still hanging out of his ear, shouting, "What happened? I wanna see!"

Telling everyone else to stay put, Father led Naser and me out to the living room. Our shoes crunched on glass shards as we inched towards the patio doors to see what carnage lay just beyond our garden wall. Out on the street, ruined flesh. A torso without a head. And blood, trickling streams of it. Puddles soaking into the pavement.

All I could do was stare as Father and Naser rushed past me to help. I pressed my temples to try to stop the ringing in my ears. The smoke and dust burned my lungs. Minutes later, Father returned, half-dragging a young man with blood spurting from his neck. Father shouted, and out of nowhere, a white scarf appeared. My mother and sisters helped the young man into the bathroom where they bound his neck as best they could. And as I just stood there watching, the stranger stared blankly at himself in the bathroom mirror. The white scarf bloomed red. My sisters fussed around him while my mother adjusted the scarf again to slow the flow of blood. Finally, he managed a smile and mumbled his gratitude.

"Bakr! Come!" I snapped to at the sound of my father's voice. Father and I helped the stranger back out onto the street and into one of the many cars waiting to help transport the wounded to the hospital. The girls followed us out and I heard one of them whisper, "He's so handsome . . ." In the distance was the wail of sirens.

That's how it was in Syria: when we heard an explosion, we ran towards the chaos. Often the police and ambulances were late arriving, if they arrived at all, so we took care of each other. After every explosion, streets were clotted with civilians doing whatever they could do to help, binding wounds, driving the worst cases to hospital.

Still dazed, I wandered back into our garden while Naser and Father remained out on the street. I nearly stepped on one of our chickens — I hadn't noticed them in all the confusion but they were all there, standing stock-still. It was like someone had hit pause when the car bomb went off. Their little black eyes blinked every so often, but their bodies were rigid with terror. The blue and green budgies, surprisingly, were chirping contentedly in their cages. The old stone wall in front of our garden was still intact, even though the section next to ours now had a gaping hole in it. My father stood there examining the crumbling wall. Months later, that same wall that had withstood a bomb blast collapsed during a windstorm.

As I refilled the water for my birds, I heard Father and Naser checking on our neighbours. Mother and my sisters were busy cleaning up all the shattered glass inside. The reporters and camera crews descended, hastily assigning blame on some rebel group or other, and behind them, the street-sweepers and the clean-up crews hurried to wash away any evidence of dissent. Eventually, the streets would be silent as everyone else hid in their homes. The chaos of the day was seeping away slowly and all I wanted to do was get back to my normal. It was Friday evening. Time to go to my cousins'.

After telling Mother where I was headed, I scurried through the back alleys to avoid the military checkpoints that dotted my neighbourhood. It wasn't safe to be in the main streets. After an attack, the place was always crawling with Assad's army or, worse yet, his *shabiha* goons. Document checks for our safety, supposedly. People were randomly questioned or even detained for hours, sometimes days. When the grenades exploded or machine guns rattled, you never knew if the attack was coming from the government or the anti-government militias that fought to control the streets of Homs. It was a continual call and answer of mortars, guns, Grad rockets, and missiles.

When I arrived at my Uncle Mohammed's apartment, I felt like myself again. I'm glad I didn't stay home that night. I'm glad I spent the night playing PlayStation with my rowdy cousins instead. On the streets outside my home, the dogs would be the final arrivals to the bloody aftermath. In the quiet of the night, strays descended onto the streets, yipping, howling, feeding.

As I strolled home the next morning, I met Amro and a few other buddies from our building. After three years of living in civil war, we had become strangely numb to the random violence that bubbled up around us.

"Hey Bakr, your family good? Where'd you go last night?" Amro's voice bounced off the walls and buildings of the quiet street.

"Yeah, everyone's fine. I was at Yousef's. You know, Friday night." I shrugged.

"FIFA 13 again? Man! Tomorrow night – my place. Rematch from Wednesday's game."

"Sure, sure." We smiled at each other and he sucked in a quick breath through his teeth. Leaning against the garden wall, we stared at the gruesome mess that remained. The corpses had been carted off but flecks of flesh and bone still stuck to the sidewalk and the walls where we hung out. The stench was overwhelming: a putrid smell that hit the back of the throat. I couldn't breathe in without tasting it. We all had our noses tucked into our collars. Sighing, I went in search of some garbage bags. Someone else retrieved a mop and bucket from home and we mopped and poured bucket after bucket of water into the street. Of course, Amro splashed water about and made stupid jokes. We elbowed each other in the ribs while we scrubbed at the bloodstains. The street slowly filled with others joining in on the effort. After a few hours, it almost seemed normal again, even though the air felt heavy with the spirits of the dead.

By the time we finished, it was late afternoon. I washed up and joined my family in the living room where they were eating and chatting. As I plopped down onto a couch, Mother cocked her head to one side and stared hard out the window. "What is that?" she asked, pointing at something snagged on the roof of the chicken coop.

Of course, Father sent me to investigate, and as I hoisted myself up on the roof, I came face-to-face with a man's jawbone. In the last year, there had been many public service announcements instructing people to bring heads or limbs that were found after attacks to the hospital or police station . . . but a jaw? I grabbed a white plastic grocery bag from the kitchen then climbed back onto the chicken coop. I plucked the jaw from the shingles and stared at it. The skin was clean-shaven and smooth. The teeth were perfectly straight. The only thing that seemed right was to give it a dignified burial. Clutching the garbage bag, I headed towards the park down the street. There, beneath a tree, just a month after my thirteenth birthday, I buried a man's jawbone.

MARCH 12, 2001, TO FALL 2010

The Sweet Life

It wasn't always like this. My life wasn't always like a scene from *Call of Duty* or *Counter-Strike*.

Actually, I was born in Iraq and we lived there until I was nine years old. When people in the West hear *Iraq*, they instantly think of Saddam Hussein and the Gulf War. But when I think about my home country, I remember the honey-drenched baklava my aunts gave me, the pinches on my cheeks, affectionate tickles under my chin, and coos of laughter. I was one of those unfortunate children always being pinched by aunties, my cheeks round and puffy like pita bread fresh from the oven. Even my best stone-faced scowl never dissuaded them — it only made them laugh harder. The only reason I didn't completely hate my cheeks was that everyone said I looked exactly like Father when he was my age.

My childhood in Iraq was a sweet one. There was laughter and joy: rich, just like the syrupy *knafa* cheese pastries I loved so much. And my red bike. It was the centre of my world. I was proud of my shiny bike, and I wouldn't let anyone else touch it or ride it, not even my older brother. Every day, I raced and weaved through the snarl of side streets to school, to Father's work, to the arcade, to the soccer field. We prayed five times a day, and every Friday, we went to mosque. I memorized the *salah* with its comforting words, and the rituals of prayer were stitched onto my very soul. I went to school and wore a blue uniform. My friends and I tore about in a pack, and we filled our time with soccer. That's what life was: friends and soccer.

In my family, there were ten people: my mother and father, three boys, and five girls. I was the third youngest. My family was crazy and loud and our home was filled with the constant chattering of my sisters, Maryam, Abeer, Aiesha, Asmaa, and

Abrar. Naser was a full ten years older than I was and, according to him, that made him the boss of me. Even though Maryam was the oldest of us kids, Naser nagged us all relentlessly, "Respect your older brother!" The baby of the family, Ali — or as we called him, Alush — was my mother's darling, but I was always closest with Father. You would expect Father to be the one to harp on me, but Father was my best friend, gently guiding me through life with patience and laughter. Both Father and Naser were tall, long-limbed, and goofy in their own ways, and sometimes it felt like I had two fathers. At least, that's what my brother wanted me to think!

Father was not like my friends' fathers. For one thing, he rarely ever yelled at us; he took the time to explain the world. But he wasn't always serious. Father loved nothing more than to tease and joke. He told everyone that his children were the light of his life. Even though my father's family was Shi'a, he raised us as Sunni. In Baserah, where we lived, the divisions between the two denominations of Islam hung heavy in the air. I felt this divide between our family and the rest of our world very early on, even though Father tried his best to insulate us from the worst of the awful, violent things people did to each other. Even so, he couldn't shield us from the whispers, the taunting, or the shunning. He couldn't ward off the disapproving grumbles of his own family; instead, he taught us to meet those painful arrows with love and acceptance, to leave it in God's hands.

I remember my first day of Grade Two. I lined up in front of my classroom with everyone else. One by one, the pock-faced teacher called our names and each child stepped up to greet him. When the teacher got to my name, I approached him and he paused and squinted hard at his clipboard. He snorted, "What kind of name is that? Abu Bakr?" and smacked me across the face. My breath caught in my chest and my cheek burned from the sting of his hand and the humiliation. Abu Bakr: a Sunni name in a Shi'a world. Gasps and giggles rippled around me. The teacher spat, "Why would your father name you that? Get inside." My lip quivered and my vision blurred but I bit the inside of my cheek hard because I didn't want to let a single tear fall. My father had taught me: no tears, no anger. I blinked and, without a word, stepped into my classroom. I was seven years old.

After school, I told Father what happened and he was furious. He marched into the school and demanded an apology. Though he got a perfunctory one, the damage had been done. Because my teacher had slapped me for no other reason than having a Sunni name, the Shi'a students felt free to tease and torment me. Every time something like this happened, Father sat me down for one of his long talks and insisted that love was the answer to this problem, that I had to push past the anger and sadness and leave all judgments to Allah. Even if everyone hated me, it was my job as a good Muslim to love them anyway. And my friends still included me in their games at recess, because really, when you're seven years old, whether you are Sunni or Shi'a doesn't matter as much as how well you play soccer.

But I wasn't the only one who was teased. My sister Aiesha was three years older than me and of my brothers and sisters, she was the most outgoing and talkative. Aiesha loved school, and her wide, black eyes sparkled as she bubbled incessantly about all the things she learned. She especially loved math and was so good at it. We used to shout numbers at her to add, subtract, multiply, and divide, and she would sing them out, like songs.

One afternoon, I came racing home for lunch and heard an angry, muffled voice. Aiesha. In hiccupping sobs, she was telling Mother that her Grade Five math teacher said she was failing and it was better that she died because she was a useless Sunni. Aiesha failing math? That didn't seem possible. She studied all the time and my parents checked her homework. I peeked into the kitchen. My mother was biting her lip, staring blankly, as Aiesha continued to sob and clutch at Mother's flowing *abaya* dress. "Why did you have to name me Aiesha? Why?"

Mother sighed. "My dear girl, leave it to Allah. There is nothing we can do about others' hatred. We can only keep our own hearts clean. Ignore them, Aiesha. Just don't listen."

Ignore them? Didn't Mother know how hard this was? But I suppose that's how it is. Kids got teased over anything so we learned to live with it, on the playground and in the streets.

It wasn't until a year later, when I was finishing Grade Three, that the situation got really serious. It felt like danger was closing in around us. There were many whispered conversations about Mother's nephew, Mithak. Mithak was twenty-five years old when his body was discovered by some neighbours in a dumpster. None of the adults talked to any of the kids about it, but when they shooed us out of the living room, we hid under the window and listened hard.

"Mithak . . . donating blood at the hospital . . .

the nurse taking his blood left the room. When she came back he was gone."

"*Ya Allah*, oh my God . . . days later . . . his body . . . dumpster . . . the syringe still in his arm."

"No wallet, no ID . . ."

"Days in the morgue . . . family . . . identify him . . ."

No one knew for sure, but Mithak's parents were certain he had been abducted by some Shi'ite fanatic who had been threatening the mosque where Mithak worked as a security guard. After what happened to Mithak, I was terrified of being kidnapped or even going anywhere near a hospital.

Father started talking about leaving Iraq, about joining the hundreds of people lined up outside the consulate offices that issued visas to leave the country. When our neighbours started to find bullets taped to their front doors, Father joined that line himself. Then, our older cousin Omar received a letter; it said his family should be beheaded because we were Sunni dogs. That's when I overheard Father whispering the word *bribe* to Mother. When a death threat that mentioned me by name arrived at our own doorstep, Father announced we were leaving.

It took months to finally get our visas, but in 2010, when I was nine, Father called us all together to announce that we were moving to a city called Homs, in Syria. My mother's mother and two brothers, Najim and Mohammed, were already there. I couldn't believe my luck. It was perfect! We were moving close to my favourite cousins and I was so excited that I didn't even really mind having to leave my red bike behind.

Our last few weeks in Baserah were a flurry of goodbyes to uncles and aunties. Everyone brought me candy. Our bus took twenty-four hours to wind its way from Iraq to Syria. We finally arrived at five in the morning and the sky was streaked with purple, pink, and orange. My father stepped off the bus, unfolded his long limbs, and breathed in the cool November morning. It was raining lightly and the air was fresh and clean. Father grinned down at me, black eyes shining. "The rain, Abu Bakr, it is a good sign."

3

A New Life

We soon became familiar with the winding streets of the ancient city of Homs. In the district known as the Old City, the native Syrians were suspicious of newcomers, but the New City was a buzzing hub of Syrians and immigrants: Sunnis, Shi'ites, Alawites, and Christians. Here, it seemed that people lived in relative harmony. Everyone smoked hookahs and slept late in the mornings. Every apartment had a cage of chirping budgies, canaries, and other little songbirds. The smoky, sizzling smells of the ever-spinning shawarma roasts were chased away by the clean, sweet breezes from Lebanon. The old and the new blended noisily in the streets: men and women in modern and traditional clothes, Arabic pop and folk songs blared from stores and apartments.

My father sold everything to move to Syria, sacrificing a successful career as a landlord. What I didn't fully understand at the time was that he gave it up so that we could have an escape route. I thought that Syria was the escape, but Father and my uncles had bigger plans.

Twenty days after our arrival in Homs, my parents took us to a grey, boxy government building. It was early and I rubbed my eyes as we stood at the entrance of a room the size of a gymnasium. "My children, Bismillah, there is an important reason why we are here today, but I will explain later. Sit quietly while I go register us first." Father gestured at the rows of wooden benches and plastic chairs and disappeared behind a partition near the entrance of the room. Still fuzzy from sleep, I lay down and tried to close my eyes but soon, Father nudged me awake. "My lazy son! Get up, Bakr! Here, hold on to this." He handed me an orange ticket.

I stared at the number on my ticket, 813. "Father? What is this? What are we doing here?"

After making sure everyone had a ticket, Father sat down on a bench facing us. "A few months ago, your uncle Mohammed applied for refugee status and we are here to do the same. I don't know if Syria will be any safer than Iraq. *Inshallah*, if God allows it, everything will be fine, but I want to make sure we have another option."

Mother, Maryam, Naser, and Abeer shifted uncomfortably while the rest of us sat there, confused. "What does that mean, Father? Refugee status?" Aiesha asked.

"Today, we are here to apply to move to a safer country, somewhere far from here. Maybe Europe, America. Remember our old neighbours, the Pachachis? I heard they are moving to Australia. We are here to meet the consulate staff so do not lose that ticket, or we're moving without you, okay?" Father's joke didn't quite land the way he wanted because we just kept staring at him.

Aiesha pressed on. "Leaving? But we just got here. I don't understand. Where are we going?"

"That will be up to Allah, my dear girl. I honestly don't know where or when. It could be months or even years. Think of this like insurance. What do you think, Abu Bakr?" Father turned to me.

"Sure, sure, Father. *Aiwa*, yes, of course, whatever you say." I tried hard to smile but looked away instead. I noticed then how crowded the room was. Why were we all trying to run away? "But Father, what about the rest of our family? Yousef? Uncle Najim? Grandmother?" I asked.

At this, Mother responded, "Of course, we are leaving together."

And so the ten of us waited together. The boredom was numbing as hour after hour passed and the morning melted into the afternoon. A large TV bolted into the upper corner of the room continuously flipped through pictures of Syria's famous ruins, and traditional Syrian music played softly on its speakers. Wandering throughout the room, I heard many Iraqi accents, but also some Somali ones. Aiesha and Asmaa went out to buy sandwiches and drinks, and I wandered the halls listlessly. Everyone who was over eighteen had to complete an intake interview, and my parents, Maryam, Naser, and Abeer practised their answers in hushed voices. Father had heard that it was important that everyone gave the same answers and he stressed that being honest was absolutely necessary. "We have nothing to hide," he kept reassuring us. One by one, the five adults went to their interviews in a separate room down the hall. I tried to follow Father into his, but the agent interviewing him paused. "I'm sorry, you cannot come in with your father," she smiled down at me, "but you can wait here." With that, she led Father into one of the many cubicles set up in the small room. I sat at the doorway and strained to hear what people were saying above the brisk clacking of keyboards.

An hour dragged by and I was numb and chilled from the linoleum floor. My mind drifted from the distant voices, to daydreams, and finally to sleep when Father gently shook me awake. He looked worn-out and relieved. "Bakr, go get everyone and bring them back here."

"Aiwa, Father," and I scrambled back down the hall towards the stuffy waiting room. Minutes later, all ten of us squeezed into an even smaller room with the woman who had interviewed Father. As she took our tickets from us, she asked us our names and ages. Alush was too shy to answer but I jumped at the chance to answer for him. Our family interview was short. The woman went on and on about the United Nations, visas, something like that. While my parents nodded intently, I daydreamed about the possibilities. What if we moved to Madrid? Then I could see my soccer hero, Ronaldo!

In the weeks following the application, my sisters and I wondered aloud about all the different countries we might end up in. We began to settle into our new home in Syria. Through December, Father and Naser struggled to find jobs and pondered possible business ideas. Maryam, who was twenty-four, blossomed. In Iraq, she led a constrained life, but here, she shed her old life as quickly as she shed her *niqab*. She began to work and train in a hair salon twice a week while the rest of us were back in school. But never mind Grade Four—my cousins were my life! Yousef, Abdil Aziz, Ali, Ibrahim, and I were always together. We were close in age—with Yousef at thirteen and Ibrahim at seven—and we played together like brothers. When we weren't kicking a ball around, we played foosball or barricaded ourselves in our rooms with our video games. We had to go to school from Sunday to Thursday, but the weekends belonged to us. We quickly developed our Friday night ritual of sleeping over at each other's houses and playing games late into the night.

Eventually, Father, Naser, and my uncles settled on opening a business of their own. Father convinced Mother to teach him how to make her chewy, soft bread. Then the men searched for the right place to open up an Iraqi bakery and I watched my older brother with envy. He had been working with Father for years ever since he refused to go back to school after he finished Grade Six.

Naser, who was chatty, charming, and bossy, became the manager of the new bakery in Homs. Just as the sun was rising, Father opened the bakery and fired up the ovens, and then Naser took over the busy morning shift. Depending on whether or not he had stayed out late with his friends the previous evening, Naser was either a brisk taskmaster or the guy lazily leaning against the refrigerator, sneaking cigarettes and joking with the employees. Once, Father caught him smoking in the bakery. He swatted the dangling cigarette out of Naser's mouth, cuffed him up the back of the head, and lectured him about bad habits while the other employees chuckled. It wasn't just the air of the bakery that was warm: the men Father hired were like family and they teased and laughed at each other. The family business started out small, but slowly, customers lined up for our bread.

I loved being at the bakery. After school ended at noon, I would eat lunch, play with my friends a little, and then head over there to help. Mostly, I did simple things like assist the customers or fetch things for the other employees, but the whole process of making bread fascinated me. It was so simple — flour, water, yeast, salt — but when you felt the dough in your hands, it came to life. It sprang

back with joy and fought while you kneaded it.
I would watch the bakers pull and stretch the
dough, tossing it back and forth, hand to hand, not
a movement wasted. The pale disc of dough would
be slapped onto the sides of the searing hot *tabun*
oven, and just as the bread started to bubble, the
baker would deftly flip it with the trusty paddle.
I loved breathing in that tangy sweetness with
a hint of smoke. Our life in Syria was much like
our bread. Crammed into our small ground-floor
apartment, we kneaded ourselves into our new life
in Homs. It was hot, hard work, but we shaped a
simple, hearty existence.

4

Wait, Wait, Little One

When I turned ten on March 12, 2011, we had been living in Homs for about four months. The atmosphere was shifting in Syria. It seemed that just as we began settling into our new life, everything else around us was stirring up. News reports were filled with words like *revolution, Egypt, oust, Arab Spring, the people*.

One Friday afternoon, I was at the prayer service at Zawiya mosque with Uncle Mohammed and Yousef. As the imam gave his sermon, everyone stood shoulder to shoulder, row by row in the main sanctuary. Eyes closed, hands folded, feet bare, hearts open. The incantations of the final prayers were rolling over the congregation in soothing, melodic waves when there was a shiver in the air. Several distinct pings and something flew by, far overhead. My eyes flew open. I knew that sound from my video games . . . bullets? My heart froze.

As I frantically craned my neck to see what was happening, glass rained down on the congregation. A voice deep inside me cried *"run"* but all I could do was stare in absolute disbelief at the rows of men around me, who kept praying as if nothing was happening. Was I imagining this? Why was no one moving? The prayer continued on.

My brain couldn't bear it. My heart pounded in my ears but even though I wanted nothing more than to run home to Father, I stayed in my place. The voices all around me kept the sanctity of the final prayer, as worshippers had done for centuries. Not a single soul broke concentration, their prayers even more intense and fervent as the bullets sung high above our heads. A quiet whimper escaped my tight throat and Yousef's eyes found mine. I clutched his arm in panic. His hand flew to clamp his mouth shut as he stifled a laugh. He stifled a laugh? We were being shot at and he was laughing?

My mouth gaped open as Yousef turned bright red with the effort of holding his snickers in.

Only when the final words of the prayer were murmured — *"Assalamu alaykum wa rahmatu-Allah"* — did anyone move. Some brushed glass shards off themselves while others sputtered in disbelief.

"What is happening?"

"Who's shooting at us?"

Shouts of *"Allah akbar!"* filled the mosque. "God is greater, God have mercy!"

"Is this some sort of accident?"

"What do we do?"

Uncle Mohammed gathered Yousef and me in his arms. "Our shoes, boys, let's go," he murmured. Out. Thank God. My whole body trembled for flight. We fumbled for our shoes and I broke into a run as soon as I slapped mine on. I was yanked back with great force. Uncle held me fast by the back of my shirt. "No! Bakr! Wait!"

"No, Uncle, no!" I gasped. Wait? There was no waiting. My mind screamed, my stomach ached, and all I wanted was home. Uncle scooped me up off my feet with one arm, like a bundle of sticks, and held me tight to his side.

"Not like that, Abu Bakr. Wait . . . wait . . ." His voice was clenched but quiet. Along with many others, we stood just outside the mosque, huddled in the cove of the front entrance. A man raced past us and I heard a gun cry out once, twice, and then a rain of shots. The man crumpled into a heap on the open street. The sky was a startling blue and the sun was unbearably bright. The entire street held its breath. Even the birds went silent. Suddenly, more people rushed out, taking their chances. Again, once, twice, and a rattle of bullets. Uncle Mohammed taught me to listen for the rhythm. Two slow, deliberate bullets. Then, a rapid volley of shots. After that, a pause as the shooter contemplated his work.

But my feet had no ears, no sense, no logic. I wriggled free, tears clouding my vision, as something wild coursed through all my veins. Two steps, and again I was choked by my collar. "Wait, wait, little one. We will do this together." I couldn't catch my breath as I stared at the man lying out in the street.

"Abu Bakr?"

I glanced up into Uncle's steady eyes and then to Yousef, whom he clutched with his other arm. My cousin nodded at me vigorously. Together, yes. We could do this together.

Uncle listened intently, head down. He gripped our hands tightly. "There," he murmured and nodded at an alley across from us. Two, three tentative steps and we were all dashing across the open street towards the cover of the building opposite the mosque. I saw nothing except the shadow of that building and, suddenly, we were in that shadow. No pause. Hands locked together, legs pumping, we followed as Uncle Mohammed led us through a labyrinth of side streets and alleys. Ronaldo or Messi couldn't have outrun us on that March afternoon.

When we finally got to the safety of my uncle's apartment, it took a long time for me to stop shaking. Aunt Ateka called Mother to let her know I was there safely and nudged a bowl of my favourite green Jell-O in my direction. I could barely swallow it down. We spent the rest of the evening glued to the TV set, trying to learn what had happened. No one had been killed in the attack and there were only minor injuries. Still, the violence against Zawiya mosque solidified the resistance that had been bubbling in Homs. Many people swore they saw Syrian president Bashar al-Assad's soldiers firing on the mosque full of people praying, a sacred space where faces, hands, feet, and souls were cleaned before being presented to Allah. The boldness of the attack angered many people and the previously quiet grumbles grew into the Arab Spring's rallying cry: "We want change!"

It took me weeks to step back into a mosque. My family tried to reassure me. They started going to a different mosque, Bilal al Habchi, and would return after Friday services saying, "See? No problem, Bakr!" But I was still rattled. If I had followed my instincts to run, it could have been me lying crumpled up in the street. What could I trust if not my instincts?

Father sat me down many times and told me that I couldn't let fear rule my life. "Life must always go on, Bakr. Death doesn't matter. Money doesn't matter. Even life itself doesn't matter, son. What matters is living your life with your family, with the people you love. We love each other, hard, and hold on tight. What we face, we face together. Together, we move forward and every little happiness we can have, we enjoy. We cannot let hatred and fear stop us from living."

I couldn't see Father's logic. Why *wouldn't* death matter? I didn't want to die. I was only ten years old. I didn't want anyone in my family to die. Death was terrifying in how random it could be. Once, a man came into our bakery and bought some bread. He went across the street to eat it in the park and was killed by a stray bullet. Finished. Death followed us into our everyday spaces, our safe spaces, and our sacred spaces. I didn't want to miss mosque, but still, I couldn't bring myself to go. In the end, Father let me take my own time.

But the shooting at the mosque had other consequences for my family. Father came back from a visit to the consulate office one evening with crushing news. Although we were now officially assigned a case number with the United Nations High Commissioner for Refugees, all applications were suspended temporarily. In the weeks that followed, there were reports of more attacks all over Syria, and the evening news was flooded with reports that country after country was issuing voluntary evacuations of its citizens and embassy personnel in Damascus. My dreams of living in Madrid and watching Ronaldo play faded.

5

APRIL TO JUNE 2011

Strange Lullaby

After what happened at Zawiya mosque, everyone
in my family was tentative. More and more
often, Mother, Alush, and even my sisters prayed
at home. Father constantly had his ear attuned
to snippets of gossip and news. As the violence
seeped throughout Homs, we watched the news
intently, searching for names of familiar places
or people, holding our breath whenever we
recognized a neighbourhood or street on the TV.

Military checkpoints and concrete roadblocks cluttered our main streets, and Father forbade us to leave home without identification documents. He even imposed a curfew: we all had to be home by *maghrib*, the prayer after the sun went down.

My mind quickly filled with the side streets and shortcuts of our neighbourhood, like the mini tactical maps in the corner of the screen in *Counter-Strike*. I knew the quickest ways and the quietest ways past the men with the guns to and from school, the bakery, my cousins' houses, the parks, the arcade, and the grocery store. You didn't have just one alternate route, you had many. My older cousins taught me to stash my beaten-up, black backpack so I could run away unimpeded by the bulkiness. Once the coast was clear, I would go back for it.

There were many whispers of neighbours and friends being interrogated by the police. People would disappear for days, only to turn up in a jail somewhere bloodied and bruised. You had to be so careful of what you said. We were afraid of saying anything in public that could be interpreted as anti-government so we started talking in code. Rather than *bombs*, we called them *flowers*. Did you see the flower in the old office building down the street? Did you hear all the flowers last night?

In even lower voices, we spoke of the *shabiha* — "ghosts" or "shadows" — a truly terrifying presence that haunted us. They weren't really ghosts, of course, just what everyone on the streets called Assad's gangs of tattooed pit bulls, pumped up on steroids and power. They weren't part of any official army but they carried big guns that were just as intimidating. Our Facebook feeds were filled with pictures of these preening thugs with their crew cuts, thick beards, and flexed biceps. If you saw one of them, it was best to silently duck into a store or alley, to become invisible.

Of course, Syrians started to push back. There were peaceful protests, mostly university students calling for national unity and true democracy. Because Syriatel — the main phone and internet company — was owned by one of Assad's rich cousins, texting out locations of rallies or using social media was out of the question. Despite that, word of planned gatherings spread rapidly. Once, in the hilly streets of Damascus, a group of anti-government protesters released thousands of ping-pong balls with the word "freedom" written on them. Assad's soldiers spent days chasing after those little bouncing balls.

The armed rebels came later. And not just one group, but many factions vying to defeat one another. Each group had its own agenda, whether political or religious. Some were progressive, secular, and democratic. Others were conservative, religious, or worse, extremist. Everyone was against the blatant cronyism and corruption of Assad's dictatorship. Regardless of who they were or what they wanted, Assad cracked down on them all without restraint.

Once, I watched a news report on a rally at Homs University. The university was in our neighbourhood and most of its students went to the mosques in our area, so I was curious to see if I recognized any of the protestors. One young woman with angry tears in her eyes kept asking, "What kind of Arabs are they? We are all Muslim brothers and sisters, so why the violence? What kind of Arabs are they?" That question echoed in my brain for a long time.

After a whole month of teasing from my family about being afraid to go to mosque, I gave in. I realized that Father was right, that while any gathering place held potential danger, we had to continue living. But when I told him I was returning, Father changed his mind. After all his efforts to convince me to return to mosque, now he was asking me to keep away for a few more weeks. Assad's police had recently been to Bilal mosque looking for a suspected rebel.

I had every intent of obeying, but when Friday arrived, Ali, Yousef, and Aziz showed up to take me to service. Father was not there to say no, and I hated being left out. So I tagged along.

When we got to the mosque and removed our shoes, I relaxed. I held peace and safety in my heart, setting my intentions for worship. Together, my cousins and I performed *wudu*, the ritual cleansing in preparation for prayer. I relished the feel of the cool water as I carefully washed my hands, mouth, nostrils, face, head, and feet. Most people were quiet as they entered the sparse, carpeted sanctuary, but here and there were low murmurs of greetings and gossip. My cousins and I joined the rows of men that were forming and soon we all basked in our familiar rituals of prayer and worship. Out of nowhere, the imam's sermon was interrupted by gunshots. Panic rose in my mouth. The entire congregation rose to its feet and chaos broke out. Frightened cries, shouted instructions, and a frenzied stampede for the stairs and doors. Somewhere outside, hidden from view, someone was firing at our mosque.

My mind blurred and I followed the mass of people stumbling towards the stairs. "My shoes! Where, where are my shoes?" I didn't think about my cousins at all. I thought only about my shoes and myself.

At the top of the stairs a big, bloated man pushed past me. He stomped down hard on my right foot and I pitched forward in pain. People surged around me and I grasped the handrail, gathering into the smallest ball possible and pressing myself against the wall. Feet thundered by, carrying a furious swirl of white tunics, flowing black skirts, and hitched-up trousers. I squeezed my eyes shut and longed for home. Why didn't I listen to Father? I held my breath and waited, my foot throbbing and refusing to run. Fear made my throat dry up. I had no idea what would happen to me.

Suddenly, I felt myself being lifted. A complete stranger cradled me tight as he carried me down the stairs but not once did he look down at me. I only remember his short-sleeved shirt with little buttons where I pressed my face against his chest. His shirt was grey-blue, like a calm, deep lake. He headed straight for the front entrance, which came bobbing into our view. Never mind shoes, we were both outside the mosque, and we joined the congregation huddling under the trees in the tiny park across the street. He finally looked at me as he carefully deposited me on the ground. His kind eyes crinkled with a quick "Are you okay?" but he didn't wait for an answer before he ran off, probably in search of his family.

Unsure of what to do, I shifted uncomfortably in my bare feet on the gravel as the congregants gathered in the park. People muttered indignantly. Some squinted at the buildings opposite the mosque, straining to see any signs of the shooter. Furious *Allah akbars* rang out. At Zawiya mosque, everyone had been so calm and insistent on holding the sanctity of our prayers. Now, after only a month of pockets of violence, we had dissolved into panicked masses. It had been possible after Zawiya to think it was a random, one-off incident, but now we felt targeted. The minutes crawled by but no more shots were fired, so the crowd slowly dispersed. Families found each other and scurried home. As the knot of fear eased, my right foot cried out for attention. But even the sharp pain couldn't distract me from my search for Ali, Yousef, and Aziz. I limped, barefoot, through the groups of people, then heard jubilant shouts of my name and saw them galloping towards me.

My cousins circled me and Aziz ruffled my hair. "Hey! What did you do, trip?" He slapped my shoulder with my dusty sandals.

"Did not!" I sniffed as I slipped into my sandals and told them what had happened.

We ambled in the direction of Uncle Mohammed's apartment and Aziz's phone rang. It was Uncle

Mohammed, telling us to pick up some fruit and drinks. Yousef and Aziz looked at each other, then down at my foot.

"Bakr, are you going to be okay walking back to our place?" My older cousins scanned me carefully. I could tell they didn't really want to leave me.

"Sure, sure. No problem." I nodded, maybe a little hesitantly.

"I'll stay with him," Ali chimed in.

"Aiwa, go. We'll be fine." This time I was much more certain. Yousef hopped onto his green bike, while Aziz balanced on the back chain stay. They disappeared down the lane.

Ali and I continued down the sidewalk when he suddenly gave an excited little yelp and knelt down.

"Look, Bakr!" He scrunched up in a little ball over his knees, peering intently into the gutter. "It's beautiful!" He picked something up and cradled it in his palm. "Cool! I've never seen one in real life before!"

I hobbled over and in his hand was a small bullet casing. It was brass and had a dull gleam to it. The bottom was bright, cherry red. "Whoa!" I breathed. It was beautiful. "Let me see!" I reached for it and Ali twisted away, running down the street.

"It's mine! Find your own!" Ali was only a few months older and we were always fighting over things.

"I'm not going to take it, you idiot!" I chased after him, everything forgotten. He stopped abruptly and knelt down again.

"Look! More!" he shouted. I caught up to him and he was right, three more casings. We looked up and down the street to see if anyone was watching: people bustled by but no one seemed to notice us. Would we get in trouble for taking these? We grabbed at them anyway and I managed to get one before Ali scooped them all up. It was cold and hard. I pocketed the casing and looked at Ali excitedly.

"I bet we can find lots more! You know where we could go?"

"Back to Bilal?" His eyebrows jumped with mischief.

"Yeah!"

We scrambled back down the street towards the mosque, our eyes glued to the ground.

"Oh! Found one!" I cried triumphantly. As we wove between people, they looked at us curiously, kids picking up bullet casings. By the time we got back to the park in front of Bilal mosque, I had a small handful. Ali rustled around in some bushes.

"There won't be any in there, stupid!" I yelled as I reached to cuff him on the back of the head. "What are you doing?"

He dodged me. "Hiding them, stupid!" he retorted as he emptied his pocket. A little pile of about ten casings nestled behind a bush. I opened my left palm to show Ali my collection then slowly shook them onto our little stash. Together we crouched down to examine our treasure. Ali jumped up. "Let's go!" The game was on.

We raced in opposite directions around the park and the mosque, scrambled down the streets, competing to see who would find more. I didn't have pockets in my shorts, so I pulled up the bottom of my T-shirt to hold them all. The casings jingled as I ran back to our hiding place and dropped them on our little pile. Ali ran up behind me and did the same. "How many? How many did you get?"

"Thirteen," I declared proudly.

"Oh. Well, I found the first four, w'Allah. So I win. Sixteen!"

"Inchibb! Shut up! Those ones don't count!" My phone pinged. A text from Uncle Mohammed: "Where are you? Are you OK???"

Whoops. Ali covered up our stash with some discarded newspapers and we jogged all the way to Uncle Mohammed's apartment. We were breathless as we bounded up the last steps. Uncle was waiting for us, unimpressed.

"What took you so long? I was worried! I was just about to send Aziz after you two," Uncle scolded. His forehead was all angry furrows.

Ali stuttered guiltily, "Bakr's foot, Uncle . . . he hurt it at the mosque so we were being slow. Sorry, Uncle." I nodded vigorously and stuck out my foot, which I had forgotten about until that moment, and started telling him how I hurt it.

Inside, while Uncle Mohammed wrapped up my bruised foot, my eyes found Ali's over the top of Uncle's head. We tried not to smile at the thought of our secret cache but Ali had to swallow a giggle.

Our game lasted about three weeks. Every time I was out in the street, my eyes were trained on the ground. I collected the casings in my pockets or backpack and whenever I was by Bilal, I checked on our growing stash. Once, Ali even found not just a casing, but an actual bullet. I kept one of the casings in my pocket for a long time. Whenever I was bored or waiting for my sisters, I liked to turn it over in my fingers, the cold metal warming up in my hands. There was nothing inside but it still had the faint smell of gunpowder and metal. One day, during a lull at the bakery, Father caught me playing with it. "Bakr, what is that?"

I hid it behind my back. "Father?"

"What is in your hand, son?"

There was no point in hiding it so I opened my palm and looked down at my shoes.

Father was calm and quiet. "Bakr. Do you know what that is?" I nodded, eyes still fixed on my runners. "Why do you have this, then?"

I stuttered, "Ali and I were collecting them. For fun. It's not dangerous, Father."

He sighed. "No, son, this one is not dangerous, but do you know what this casing means? It means someone shot a gun. They shot at another person. That bullet might have hurt someone, or killed someone."

My eyes met his and I could tell he was upset, despite his calm tone. I had never thought of it that way.

"Bakr, I don't want you playing with this anymore. I don't want any of these in our home, in the bakery. This is not who we are."

I nodded and dropped the casing into his open palm. I hadn't meant to upset Father: it was only a collection. I didn't think it was fair that I was getting in trouble over garbage.

"Bakr, I just want you to think about what those bullet casings mean." Father was insistent and I could tell it was serious to him.

"Okay, Father, *aiwa*."

That was the only time we talked about it. I didn't go back to our secret stash, not so much because Father forbade it, but because it had lost its magic. There were casings all over the place — nothing new or special to them anymore — and I slowly realized what that meant. They were everywhere because we heard those guns all the time now.

As the weeks slipped by, we heard more and more gunshots. Worse yet, there were different sounds rumbling through the nights. I remember the first night it happened. We were already in bed, around ten. I shared a room with Naser and he was snoring steadily. At first, I thought I heard the whistle of Naser's snoring. It sounded not far and not near but just loud enough to hear it. Suddenly, there was a crash and a shudder, and I sat straight up in bed. Naser jolted awake too. He jumped out of bed, "You hear that?" his eyes wide and unbelieving. Muffled, I heard Alush crying across the hall in my parents' room where he slept. I could hear my sisters' panicked voices as we all snapped on the lights. Father came rushing out, pulling on his robe, only one slipper on his feet. "No! Lights off!" he barked as he rushed towards the windows facing the street.

Naser pounced on the light switch as I sat in bed dumbly watching him. "Shh!" he hissed into all the bedrooms as he joined Father. I leaned over to see if I could look into my parents' room where I could hear Alush whimpering softly, but it was too dark. My sisters' bedroom door was closed.

Silence, then abruptly, the clatter of a machine gun. More silence, then the shuffle of Naser's bare feet. He came back into our room, his cellphone lighting his way. "We can't see anything. But there's no one in the street. Must be a few blocks away. Al Shammas, probably." Al Shammas was the neighbourhood adjacent to ours, and there had been months of demonstrations and protests there. Here in Akrama, posters and murals of Assad were everywhere and the only demonstrations were the ones the government organized and televised. We never went to these gatherings, on Father's orders. But Father did put up a framed photograph of President Assad in front of our cash register at the bakery. As he did it, he gave me a mischievous wink and said, "Insurance."

Naser rubbed his forehead sleepily and yawned. "It's probably nothing. Go to sleep, Bakr." He flopped back onto his single bed and I still sat in my own, mouth hanging open. Go back to sleep? How? I wanted to be with Father, but I was too afraid to leave the safety of my blanket. "Naser, where's Father? . . . Naser?"

"Living room window." His grumble was muffled by his blanket.

I pulled my blanket up around my chin even though the June night was warm. I slowly eased myself back down into bed, staring up at the ceiling, ears straining.

I heard a door open slowly. "Mom? Dad?" It was Maryam, whispering. I sat up, trying to see out of the crack of our door. Nothing. I heard the lopsided shuffle of a slipper on the floor and Father's even voice.

"It's nothing we need to worry about, Maryam. There's nothing I can see. Our street is quiet. No one has passed by. Go back to sleep, it's okay. Tell your sisters." My sisters' door softly closed then my father's head popped in and he smiled gently at me. "I knew you'd be up. Don't worry, Bakr. I don't see anything out there. It's not us. I'm going to sit up and watch for a little while, but I don't think we need to worry. Go to sleep. I'll come get you if I see anything, okay?" His head was gone again, but I could hear his soft voice across the hall telling Mother the same thing.

As I slid back into bed, I noticed Naser's breathing was heavy. I couldn't understand how he could be sleeping already. The pounding of my heart slowed but my throat was still so dry and my stomach was cramping. My t-shirt clung damply to me. Our alarm clock ticked steadily on, but I wasn't any closer to sleep. I knew Father was out in the living room, on his silent watch.

About half an hour passed, and then "TAHhhh!" A short, sharp crack. "TAHhhh!" Next, the staccato crashing of machine guns. Several beats, then the shrill scream and quake of a falling shell. Something inside me leapt up and without thinking, I was out of bed. I ran for Father and nearly crashed into him. I clutched onto him helplessly, without caring how babyish it seemed. His big hand rubbed my back. "It's okay, son. Look." I buried my face even further in his robe. "Look, Bakr, in the street. Do you see anything?" He shook me gently. A quiet minute dragged by. "Look, son. See the street?"

Finally, I turned my head slowly. I saw our birdcages. The garden wall. The street lamp across the street.

"See, nothing! It's okay. No problem! Probably Al Shammas again . . . Okay, Bakr?" I looked up at him. "To bed!" He gently shoved me in the direction of our bedrooms. "I'm coming too. Let's go."

That was the first night of the strange lullaby.

From then on, we heard it more frequently, sometimes frighteningly close. It was my best friend, Amro, who discovered exactly how close those cracking gunshots were. Amro's family lived in the same building as we did, and late one evening, Amro was lost in his thoughts carrying the garbage down to the dumpster. As he rounded a corner on the landing of the stairs, he practically ran into a stern-faced soldier who had a sniper rifle slung casually on his back. Amro turned and flattened himself awkwardly against the bannister wall, as if willing himself to disappear. He admitted he nearly wet his pants. The soldier passed Amro, his focus elsewhere. That's how we discovered the army snipers liked to set up on our building's rooftop. That's how close those horrible pops in the night were. Sometimes, a few weeks would pass by in silence, but then we'd have night after night of that terrifying lullaby.

"TAHhhh!" sings the sniper rifle.

"Ra-tat-tat-tat-tat-tat-tat-tat!" The chorus of machine guns.

Then, the soprano screech and baritone tremor of the mortars.

After a while, we learned to fall asleep to it.

6

My First Massacre

Over the next year, the violence settled, uneasily, into the background hum of our daily life, which for me meant video games and Grade Five. The covered shopping arcades still buzzed with Arabic pop and the chatter of birds and parrots. People smoking hookahs shouted at each other as friends strolled by. Children continued to taunt and shriek as they dashed in and out of the crowds of shoppers. But now, there was a note of tension — everyone was on the lookout for the ever-increasing numbers of men in uniforms.

One day, we were all gathered in the living room finishing off our lunch. Abeer was just tidying up while Aiesha and Asmaa were texting on their phones. Maryam and I were watching TV when Father cleared his throat to get our attention. "Okay, my family, I have something important to say. This . . . craziness isn't going away anytime soon. It seems like every week there are more checkpoints and soldiers in our streets, and I think it will get far worse before it gets better." He paused. "I know this is not what we are taught is right, but from now on, if anyone stops you and asks, tell them you are Shi'a." Aiesha and I looked at each other. With our Sunni names, we knew, better than our other siblings, how being Sunni had marked us for scrutiny, ridicule, and sometimes even danger. Father continued, "It is wrong to lie and I am not ashamed to be a Sunni, but I think for safety's sake, if the *shabiha* or a soldier ever asks, just take the easy lie." I knew it was no easy thing for Father to tell us to lie; however, our safety was more important. I often heard him saying to Mother or my uncles, "What will tomorrow look like for my family? How do I protect my children?" Many nights, when I woke up for a glass of water, I would catch a glimpse of Father at the window, listening like an animal on alert to the noises and shouts in the dark streets.

Father took even more precautions for my sisters. We didn't even have pictures of them on our phones: Father forbade it. When the soldiers or *shabiha* stopped to check our IDs, they would often take our cellphones and look through our pictures, asking about the people in them. Weeks before, Father had had us change our cellphone wallpaper to the Syrian flag. Sure, that home-screen made the soldiers take on a friendlier tone, but they still questioned us too much for comfort. Any encounter with a soldier was terrifying because you never knew if he was going to try to make your life miserable, do a document check, or just ignore you. The danger was random. You never knew what could get you in trouble. Your name? Religion? The way you glanced at the man? It was better to avoid any contact. Father said he didn't want the army to know anything about Mother or my sisters. As a further precaution, he insisted that they were always accompanied by Father himself, Naser, or me.

Of course, I knew it was important but *Ya Allah*, the shopping felt endless! I would arrive home with Abeer, lugging her bags, and Aiesha and Asmaa would screech at me from the door for not taking them too. Father would snicker at me from behind his newspaper as my sisters whined until

I agreed to take them the next day. Aiesha tugged me into store after store. "Which jacket do you like? The brown one or the white one?"

I rolled my eyes. A mistake.

"Hiff! Have more of a fashion sense, Bakr! Tell me! Which one?"

A sigh. "Fine. That brown one, *aiwa*," I pointed, barely looking up from my cell.

A collapse of giggles. It was a trick question. "Bakr! Gross! You have no style at all!" Shopping, always shopping, my sisters. I could never understand what they had to buy all the time!

Another task that often fell to me was accompanying my Grandmother Maryam but, unlike shopping with my sisters, I rarely minded. Grandmother was warm like the sun, always laughing and telling stories, her henna-stained hands dancing for emphasis. My sisters were especially close to her and they often sat together weaving mats and fans, in the traditional way. Although she lived with Uncle Najim and his family, she often visited our apartment and Uncle Mohammed's: "keeping an eye on those lazy grandkids," as she put it. She was nearly seventy-five years old but she didn't let anything slow her down. Except the army. Because she was so scared of the soldiers at the checkpoints, every time she wanted to come over, she would call and one of us boys, usually me, would pick her up.

On one of those walks together, we were arm in arm and Grandmother was chatting about her neighbour, when the air seemed to vibrate. It was such a strange, new feeling that we paused to listen. I was trying to figure out what kind of an engine would make that fluctuating, growling noise when suddenly two fighter jets blew by overhead. The roar of the engines was deafening and I'm not sure if it was me that was shaking or the ground. I clutched onto my grandmother and she onto me and we hit the pavement together. We stayed huddled on the sidewalk as the roar receded and all I could hear was our shaky breath. My stomach cramped violently and I squeezed my eyes shut to stop the tears from coming. After a few moments, I felt her hand rubbing my back. "Bakr, look, we're nearly home, let's go," and she helped me up.

"Bakr, it's okay. It scared me too. Don't be ashamed, dear boy." I shyly glanced back at her as she chuckled and wiped the smudges from her kohl-rimmed eyes. "See? No one has to know." My grandmother knew my heart so well.

We walked the last block home in silence. We never spoke of it to anyone but I knew, by the way my grandmother gripped my hand, that she was terrified of those fighter jets too.

Actually, it was Grandmother who taught me how to deal with my fear. We could tell she was especially anxious when she would start cleaning everything, even things that were cleaned just yesterday. Grandmother kept herself distracted with chores or tending to our garden.

So, no matter how much the gunshots or explosions rattled me, I would clench my teeth and try to find that peaceful place inside. Praying helped. So did soccer. Father talked to me a lot. Video games were a way of forgetting. Father told us that it was important not to let the war scare us out of living.

At the dinner table or around the TV, Mother would bring up Iraq. The violence, gunfire, and helicopters were getting to her, as they were for all of us. One day, after another news report, she turned to my father and told him she wanted to return to Iraq. Father sighed and switched the TV off.

"No, Nihad. Iraq is not our answer. If I die, I will die in Syria, not Iraq."

Mother's eyes flared with frustration.

"Nihad, be patient. Everyone, listen to me. We have to be patient. I will never return because Iraq will never be our safety."

70

"Hafedh," Mother bristled, "*hiff* . . . are we really any safer here?"

"The UN," Father began, "I refuse to give up on that hope. I've been calling the agency every month. The office only accepts phone calls on Tuesdays and Wednesdays but . . ." He sighed and turned to Mother. "Nihad, it is our only safe option. Think of it: America, maybe Canada. There, we will grow stronger together. We will be free. We can lead a happy, new life. No helicopters." We all knew how much my mother despised the chopper blades beating the air. It's a sound that you feel deep inside your body. It almost follows your own steady heartbeat, but the way the blades pound the air, your heart can't help but race to follow it.

Mother exhaled and Father turned again to the rest of us. "We can make a home anywhere we go together."

MAY 15, 2012. Our whole family, along with Father's friend Aarif, Grandmother, and Uncle Najim's family, crowded into our apartment. My younger cousins, Raiyan, Islam, and Maram, played with Abrar and Alush while the rest of us picked at the remnants of lunch.

Cups of steaming, spiced black tea loaded with sugar were being passed around when gunshots rang out. Everyone paused and listened but they sounded far away. A beat or two of silence, then machine guns. Instinctively, we moved away from the windows and Uncle Najim drew Raiyan into his lap as she nuzzled down into her father's shirt. Grandmother turned to her tea and sipped quietly. Rat-tat-tat-tat-tat, about ten minutes' worth. When the shots finally subsided, Father nodded at me. Since I was closest, I inched towards the window and peered out the side of Mother's green curtains that were waving in the breeze. Outside on the street, nothing unusual, only traffic. A woman on her cellphone strolled by, her arms full of grocery bags.

I turned back towards the room and shook my head. Uncle Najim shrugged and the men continued their conversation. Cutlery and dishes continued to clink and my cousins un-paused their video game. More cups of tea.

I couldn't shake that feeling in my gut. I returned to the couch but my eyes darted to the window every few minutes. Ali playfully slapped me upside the head and laughed at me. "So serious, Bakr!"

Father shook his head gently at me, smiling. Something caught my eye out the window. Actually, it wasn't *something*, it was *nothing*. Suddenly, there was nothing outside, not a soul, not a car on the usually busy street. I stood, attention trained outside and then, loud pops of gunfire. This time, it sounded a lot closer and we heard the call and response of several rifles. A few small explosions, far away. Father's friend shot up from his armchair, hastily mumbled thanks and something about his family, and rushed out the garden door before anyone could stop him. The TV blinked out.

My older cousin, Abdullah, picked up the phone. "Phone's dead."

"Internet too," Maryam's voice rang out as she snapped her cellphone shut.

The rumbling stampede of army boots on the pavement had us in full retreat to the back bedrooms. Father gently closed the hallway door that separated the two halves of the apartment and there we stayed, waiting for all the sounds to subside. How do you pass time like this? Video games played on mute. Quiet gossip about schoolmates and neighbours. A nap, maybe. By the third hour, everything sounded normal outside. There had not been any shots in a long time, so Abdullah and I snuck out into the garden to see what was going on.

Outside, Abdullah and I ducked behind the garden wall and cautiously peered over top. What we saw was a huge army truck, with men in uniforms hanging out the open back doors, grabbing and hitting people as the truck slowly rumbled down the street. Abdullah and I turned to each other, adrenaline pumping.

"They're going to come for us! They'll come inside —" I gasped. Before Abdullah could answer, Father and Uncle Najim hissed at us to come back inside. They, too, had seen the army trucks in the streets. We ducked back in, leaving the chickens and budgies to their blissful cooing.

Back inside, my father was stammering something. Again, we packed ourselves into three bedrooms. Father looked at me as I entered his room, dread filling his normally calm eyes. "Aarif. I can't believe I let him leave. Why did I let him leave? Why did I invite him over for lunch?" His eyes flicked to his cellphone in his hand. No service. "*Inshallah*, by the grace of Allah . . ." A quick prayer for Aarif's safety. I had never seen Father so afraid before, and watching him agonize over his friend was worse than my own fear. He sat on the bed. He paced. He listened by the hallway door. He glanced, constantly, at his phone, waiting for the reassuring bars to appear, signaling cell service. Occasionally, machine gun fire punctuated the growing night but an uneasy silence slowly settled over the neighbourhood.

Around nine, our home phone rang and we all jumped. Father dove for the cordless and let out a loud sigh. It was Aarif, and he was home safe. Apparently, he had woven through the back alleys to avoid the roving patrols. As he scrambled over a back wall, he was stopped, but it was just a document check and he was released without any problems.

Rather than face the streets at night, Uncle Najim's family stayed over, everyone a bit shaken from the day. Mother and Aunt Muna took to the kitchen and soon the reassuring smell of baking bread wafted through the apartment, mingling with the voices of my cousins laughing and Al Jazeera blaring from the TV. My father sat on the sofa, absorbed in the news, the tension of the day slowly sliding off him. My mother brought out another plate full of steaming sesame bread.

"Nihad, the smell of your bread is going to bring soldiers knocking on our door!"

She snorted in mock contempt and suppressed a laugh, the light dancing in her eyes. She shook her head and I swear she muttered, "Hiff . . . the UN," under her breath.

The next morning, over a silent breakfast, we heard the news. Al Shammas: an unknown number of dead in the streets and hundreds arrested.

Rumours of people being doused in fuel or prodded with live electric cables. We didn't know what was true or false but no horrible act seemed impossible now. My first massacre.

7

And Then a Second One

On a stifling Friday night in August, Aziz, Yousef, and I took turns beating Ali at FIFA 13. To drown out Ali's whines about switching to *Grand Theft Auto* instead, Aziz sang and rapped about whatever popped into his head. All of us laughed at them. Elbows in the ribs, slaps on the back, eyes dry and tired from staring at the screen too long.

In the morning, my eyes were still heavy with sleep as I shuffled out to the living room, in search of some water. My fuzzy brain registered Uncle standing in the window. From the fifth floor, he had a good view of the neighbourhood below.

My footsteps must have startled him because when he turned, panic was still on his face. That's when I registered the shouts below and the faint popping of gunshots. I joined Uncle at the window and saw the swarms of uniforms in the streets about two blocks away. Men, sometimes even women, were pulled out of their buildings, some still in their pyjamas. The *shabiha* roamed about in hungry packs, like mad dogs, barking out insults and orders. Here and there were muffled shouts, thrown punches, shouting women, crying children, more gunshots. There were the distant screams of Grad rockets and explosions.

Uncle eased the wooden shutters of the window shut while I closed the other set. He rushed to alert the rest of the family. "Shh . . . quiet, quiet, everyone . . ."

Inside Yousef and Aziz's room, I fumbled around for my cellphone. When I flipped it open, it was blank. No service. Instinctively I patted my pockets for my documents. *Ya Allah.* My ID. Where?

"Yo, Bakr, what's wrong?" Yousef peered at me, his black hair pointing in all directions.

"My documents. Did you see them? Did you?"

Father would be furious. Had I forgotten them at home? Were they in this room somewhere? Did I lose them? Without answering, Yousef started rifling through the room while Aziz went to search the apartment. I slumped onto the bed and squeezed my head between my hands.

"Oh my God, Bakr . . ." Yousef breathed. This was bad. If I was stopped by a soldier and didn't have my identification papers on me, they could assume anything about who I was or where I was from. They could hold me for as long as they wanted and my family might not even know I was taken.

Aziz returned, head shaking. He flopped down beside me and punched me in the arm. "Stupid!"

Yousef chortled, "Ziz, look how pale he is." Snorts of laughter and more punches.

"*Inchibb!* Shut up, shut up! I know! How do I fix this?" I pleaded.

My cousins both shook their heads dumbly at me. Best-case scenario, the papers were at home. Worst-case scenario, I lost them on the street somewhere. I looked down at my useless phone again. The sounds of the fighting and commotion out on the street were unbearable. In raids like these, it wasn't unusual for the army to go from home to home, looking for suspected rebels. This last week ten rebels — maybe more — had been publicly executed by the police. Beaten to death as their neighbours watched. Beaten with hammers. This was not the time to be anywhere without identification. My stomach seized with cramps.

We snuck out into the living room to try calling on the landline. Beep, beep, beep. Busy tone. Nothing to do but wait. The day crawled by while we hung out in the back bedrooms. No matter how many times we picked up the phone, all the landlines were jammed and busy. No cell service. A quiet, cold lunch of day-old bread, hard-boiled eggs, yogurt, and milk. Everyone listened for the sound of army boots on the apartment steps, but thank Allah, they never came. Finally, around seven that night, Uncle Mohammed got through to Father on the landline. Everyone was safe. Uncle called me to the phone and Father's voice rumbled through the line.

"Hey Bakr. Where are your documents?"

I swallowed hard. "Father?"

A chuckle. "Relax, my son. They're here. Oh my God, how stupid you are! Don't do that again."

"Aiwa, Father, I'm sorry." My cheeks burned with embarrassment and relief.

"I know," came his reassuring voice. "Listen, there's still a lot of shooting around here. Something must be going down in Al Shammas again. Stay at

Uncle's tonight. Play your silly video games, okay? I'll call you tomorrow."

A click. My uncle smiled at me and nodded his head towards my cousins' room. On the TV was the familiar green field and the little players sprinting back and forth. Aziz and Yousef were glued to the screen, mouths hanging a little open, elbows up and jousting each other every few moves. Ibrahim bounced on the bed, clutching a pillow and shouting commentary, instructions, and insults. I plopped happily on the bed and shoved him gently. This spurred an attack of giggles and punches, which was the best way to block out the intermittent gunshots that popped through the night.

When most people hear *massacre*, they picture body bags and blood. But this was what massacres felt like for me: the tense, stale air of a bedroom with too many breathing bodies in it. Finding quiet ways to pass the frightful hours, trying your best to block the sounds from flooding your brain. I've seen the YouTube videos of massacres that happened while I hid in those bedrooms. The picture, grainy from someone's camera phone, so bouncy and uneven that it almost gives you motion sickness watching it. Here a foot, there a head, blood splatter everywhere, the sounds of

wailing women. Or a room where bodies were
stacked, two, three high, like sacks of flour. An arm
or foot sticks out. A woman's torn hijab. Always
shoeless feet. Where do all the shoes go? Images
like these were beamed out into the world, the
people pleading, "See? See what they're doing?"
The various rebel groups and government accusing
the other of more senseless violence, completely
missing the point that all this violence was senseless. The rest of us were caught helplessly between
two, three, ten fighting sides.

Massacres, to me, were the terrifying, muffled
sounds outside those closed bedroom doors. But
this second massacre was different. The following
morning, I met my uncle in front of the shuttered
living room window.

"Uncle . . . I want to see."

He looked at me for a long time. Does he keep
his eleven-year-old nephew from witnessing or
does he allow him to know the truth? "Bakr . . .
okay. But if I tell you to step back from that
window, you do it right away. Promise?"

"Yes, Uncle."

Uncle Mohammed motioned me to peep
through the side cracks rather than opening the
shutters. Together, we looked out at the corpses
lying in the street when suddenly, Uncle gave a

start. With shocking speed for such a big guy, he
threw open the front door and thundered down
the apartment stairs. "Stay there!" he called back
over his shoulder, all quiet and caution abandoned.
I peered back through the shutters to see him in
the street, kneeling next to a man with a beard and
stained *taqiyah* cap clinging to his head. Several
other men already out in the street cleaning joined
my uncle by the still body. One of them flagged
down a passing car and the three strained to get
the man into the car. I watched Uncle shut the car
door. The way his right hand clutched his mouth
as his shoulders quivered. That was not my first
time seeing a corpse, but it was the first time I
recognized one: Hassan, a man I had often seen at
the mosque laughing with my uncles and Father.

LATER THAT AFTERNOON, on my way to the
bakery, I was alarmed to see so much new destruction on our street. As I walked down the middle
of the carless street, I noticed the top corner of
Sayid's barber shop, where I got my hair cut, had
been blown off. Was he okay? The city was disinte-
grating before us. A dented, yellow dumpster full
of busted-up concrete sat beside the sidewalk, in
front of our bakery. "Bakr! Get out of the street!

Use the sidewalk!" My father stood outside, flour all down the front of his shirt, gesturing wildly with a dishtowel.

Before I could move, I heard the pop of a gun and loud metallic bangs as bullets hit the dumpster in front of me. I lunged for cover and scrambled behind a parked car. Father ducked behind a sign and his eyes bore into mine. I could tell he wanted to call out to me but he knew better. I looked down at myself frantically and patted my chest, sides, legs. I shook my head at him because I knew his question. We froze and listened. Nothing. Father slowly stood up, looking cautiously over the top of the sign while I peeked down the street in the direction where the bullets had come from. Nothing other than a few other bewildered people, crouched behind whatever cover they could find. Father dashed towards me, hunching his tall frame, and he was beside me in a few steps. He grabbed me by the shoulders and scanned me with a sharp eye. "Are you sure you weren't hit, Bakr?"

"What was that?"

He didn't bother answering but whisked me into the bakery and slammed the rolling metal shutters. It took a week before we decided to tell Mother. We knew she wouldn't handle it well, even though I wasn't hurt.

A few weeks later, I went back to that yellow dumpster. My fingers traced the bullet holes in the side of it. There was even part of a slug partially wedged into the metal. It seemed so strange to think that one of those bullets could have found its way into me. What had I done? Why did someone shoot at me? I was only a kid. What if it had been Alush and he didn't know to duck behind something? He would have just crouched down into a little ball in the street. What if it was one of my cousins, earphones in, too absorbed in music to hear the shots?

I stalked down the street, kicking at rocks and rubble, when something caught my eye. A bullet, a big one. A round from an AK-47. This wasn't just a casing, but an actual bullet. I picked it up: icy cold. A bullet as long as my palm with a fierce tip. I imagined it tearing into my flesh and a shiver ran through me. I remembered Father's words. These things *weren't* us. My cheeks burned in shame at the thought of how Ali and I had actually collected them a year ago. Suddenly, I hated this thing in my hand. It was the reason I couldn't play soccer in the street anytime I wanted. It was the reason I couldn't go to my friend's house because there was shooting in his neighbourhood. As much as Father wanted us to believe we could

keep living our lives, it wasn't true. He was wrong.
We couldn't pretend this war wasn't happening.
There were rules to follow, dangers to avoid.
I hated that bullet so much in that moment, the
seething anger blurred my eyes.

I couldn't stand the feel of this terrible thing
in my hand but I also didn't want to just drop it
back in the street. What if another child found it
and kept it? Or what if someone else found it?
The army had begun offering five lira for every
intact bullet that was turned in. There was no way
it was going to the army. I shoved the bullet in
my hoodie pocket and walked back towards the
dumpster, made sure no one was looking, then
pitched it in. There was a satisfying clang as it
rattled to the bottom of the bin. No one would find
it now. It couldn't hurt anyone. It would just be
buried at the dump along with smelly diapers and
rotten fish heads.

8

Damascus

For once, I was excited for the start of the school
year because I was going into Grade Six and I
couldn't wait to finish elementary. Next year,
I would go to the junior high school across the
field where Aiesha and Asmaa went.

That September morning began like it usually
did: I was waiting for my sisters so we could walk
to school together. Father telephoned from the
bakery. "Bakr, I want you to be extra careful at
school today. Be alert, son. Last night, a policeman

was killed by a car bomb a block from your school. One of the customers that came in this morning said that the army has been firing rounds in the air to scare people. Watch your sisters carefully, okay? Make sure you all have your documents. No daydreaming. No hanging around. Take your sisters straight to school and go straight home after, okay?"

"Of course." I nodded even though I knew he couldn't see me.

Aiesha and Asmaa strolled and gossiped. I followed them on my bike, my mind full of soccer team tryouts. Would I make the team? I needed to work on my deking. As we approached the school, I shushed them and tried to focus on my surroundings. We were across the street from the school, and I was trying to pick my friends out of the clumps of kids in the sea of blue uniforms, when an explosion shattered the peace of the morning. My sisters and I ducked down behind a parked car to avoid the rolling cloud of dust. When it passed us, I looked for the blast site. Two, maybe three blocks down the street from our school, smoke and fire billowed out of a shell of a car. Terrified screams and parents running around crying in anguish. My sisters looked at me and I breathed, "GO!"

I hopped off my bike so they could keep up with me. I led, they followed, their hands gripped tight and backpacks bouncing wildly. No main streets. We ducked and dodged through alleys, courtyards, and side streets. The object was to avoid the army: after a bombing like this, they would arrest anyone, even children. In Darra, the government arrested and publicly beat a few kids for anti-government graffiti, so, no — not even children were safe from the army.

Ten breathless minutes later, we were home, gasping for air but safe. Mother swept us into the apartment, muttering, "Alhamdulillah, thank God," under her breath.

A few days later, fighter jets dropped bombs close to our school. "To flush out violent rebels," the news reports said. Thankfully the two schools were closed so no one was hurt, but my elementary school was destroyed. The elementary kids had to go to the junior high school and in that twisted way, I got my wish of going to junior high.

For weeks after, Mother clenched her hands in constant worry. The circles under her eyes deepened, and her eyes were always puffy from tears she hid from us. Sometimes, while we did our homework in the living room, we'd hear snippets of whispered conversations behind my parents' closed door, Mother begging for a break from the bombs. In the early days, Father had tried to calm her with some mention of the UN, but after nearly two years, even he was giving up on that dream. For two years, he had been calling the consulate office every month and now even the visa officer hinted that there was very little hope. It was strange to see Father so dejected. It was even more surprising to see Naser take the phone number from him. "Okay, no problem, Father. *Bismillah*."

From then on, Naser called religiously. Every Tuesday during his morning break at the bakery, Naser would phone and explain our situation. Of course, because you never knew if your calls were being monitored, Naser would speak in vague terms. He couldn't say, "We are in danger and need to leave," because that might sound like anti-regime talk. Instead, "You know how it is in Homs, things are difficult. Our file number is . . ." His friends teased him because Naser repeated the exact same thing every week, to the point where it sounded like a script or a prayer. Abdil Karim, one of our most trusted employees, joked that the office staff must know Naser's voice by now.

But as time passed and the violence in Homs seemed only to get worse, Father, Uncle Najim, and Uncle Mohammed came to a decision: we were all moving to Damascus, the capital of Syria. It was a bigger city than Homs, and Assad's sights weren't trained on it the same way they were on Homs. At least Damascus hadn't been in the news as much and Naser had been back and forth for business and visits with friends without incident. Hasty preparations were made. We had no idea how long we would be gone, or if we were coming back to Homs at all. Out, Mother just wanted out.

The plan was made. Uncle Najim and Father would go ahead to Damascus with all of us in tow, and Uncle Mohammed and his family would follow a few weeks later, once all loose ends were tied up.

SIX IN THE MORNING. The Levant winds were blowing, the October air crisp and sharp, and we had a minibus to load. Our collection of suitcases, duffle bags, and red-white-blue nylon canvas bags was piled in the courtyard, nestled against the empty chicken coop and birdcages. The minibus driver chain-smoked cigarettes, nervously rubbing his hands against the cold and craning his neck around every few seconds. He had parked down the block, as far as he could from a nearby military checkpoint. Of course, he was right to be paranoid because you never knew what kind of attention a move like ours would attract. Father, Naser, and I silently loaded up the bus as quickly as possible.

As Naser grabbed the last few bags, he froze in place and made a low whistle. He pointed down the cross street with his eyes. Father and I peered around the corner and saw two tanks with their main guns pointed at a sharp angle up into the sky, a common tactic of the army to intimidate people. The tanks were slowly rumbling down the street in our direction, so the only thing we could do was flee. We ran home and hid until the rumble of caterpillar tracks on pavement subsided.

Once the tanks were gone, we loaded the last of the bags. There was a flurry of hijabs and *abayas* as my sisters scurried into the minibus. Father gave the driver instructions to drive to Najim's apartment so we could load them up and head out, but was met with furious head-shaking. The tanks had rattled the driver and he now refused to drive to Najim's because doing so would take him past several checkpoints. A sigh, a phone call on Father's cell, and a new plan: the family, and all their bags, would have to come to us.

It would look too suspicious for the whole family to travel as a pack with their bags. With some quiet organization, the men began ferrying

Najim's bags to the van, and my cousins came
over a few at a time to board the waiting vehicle.

We were nearly in the clear when a pair of army
officers came to sniff out what was going on. We
had passed them one too many times. But Father
was good with officers. He was calm, assertive, and
deferential enough not to rouse any hostility. He pro-
duced his documents and explained in an even voice
that the whole family was moving to Damascus.

One of the men waved Father's documents away.
"Sure! A fine day for a move! Pull your van up.
We'll help." A toothy smile.

Father pressed his lips into a smile and nodded
his head ever so slightly. "That is kind. Thank you."

"We'll meet you up at that checkpoint." The
shorter officer pointed with his gun that was slung
over his shoulder and resting in front of him.

We were still frozen where we had been standing when the soldiers first approached. We all
exchanged hesitant glances; it felt like a trap.
"In," Father gestured. Gently, Abeer and my cousin
Haneen helped Grandmother into the van and
we piled in around her, the soft musky smell of
her perfume making that cramped van slightly
less horrifying.

Abdullah and Naser hastily jammed the last bags
into the bus and piled in along with everyone else.

The driver, white-knuckled, pulled the bus up. My sisters broke into an uneasy chatter, trying to sound nonchalant. Finding it oddly quiet in the back, I turned to check on Raiyan, Islam, Maram, Abrar, and Alush huddled together in the last row of seats, wide-eyed and silent. I nodded at them reassuringly. The bus slowly crept towards the knot of uniforms. No other vehicles were there. We waited in tense silence. All talk of the weather had gone stale.

While the stockier officer slowly circled us, the tall one with the toothy smile approached the passenger side where Father was seated, his hands gripping all of our IDs. "Okay, just give us a moment. Damascus, right?"

Father nodded. Before Father could even hand over our documents, the officer strolled back into the checkpoint booth where there was a lot of talking and nodding at a phone. I finally gathered the nerve to look up from my shoelaces and my gaze accidentally met the soldier's. His stalking-animal eyes bore into mine as he smiled his dead smile. The warmth drained from my body and my eyes darted back to my shoes. I willed myself to look back up. It seemed safer, somehow, to keep an eye on him. That officer stared us down the whole time, shuffling his feet and kicking the dust as he walked the length of the bus. The entire time he circled us, he kept his AK-47 cradled in front of him, the rifle sling over his left shoulder, his left hand on the wooden fore-grip, his right hand on the pistol grip. Deliberately, his right forefinger toyed with the fire selector lever. Up, safety on. Centre, fully automatic. Down, semi-automatic. Centre, up, centre, down, centre, up, centre, down. That smile. Click, click, click, click. I could not tear my eyes away from the selector lever. Click, click, click, click. My breathing was shallow and I heard my father and my uncle in my head: "Wait, wait." That sickening smile again. Fifteen torturous minutes clicked by.

Finally, the tall soldier sauntered back. He looked at Father, peered in at the rest of us, huffed, and cracked a fake smile. "Okay, you're good to go." He patted the hood of the bus, stepped back, and nodded at his partner. Father was so stunned that he started to wave our documents at the officer but the driver peeled away before anyone noticed. Father turned back at us as we merged onto the busy main street, the panic and surprise on his face as clear as day. Through, we were through. Nervous laughter rippled through the van.

The rest of the ride was a bumpy, boring three-hour affair on the Damascus–Aleppo highway.

The crumbling buildings of Homs gave way to wheat and barley farms. Ragged cotton fields and olive groves turned into expanses of dusty desert, then into the hills and plateaus around Damascus. I wish I could say it was relief that I felt as we rolled into the City of Jasmine, but the streets, crammed with people who never made eye contact, felt cold and alien.

Perhaps the only bright spot about living in Damascus was that now we lived in the same building as my cousins. We were the only occupants in the cramped, four-storey walk-up. The ground floor storefront was shuttered and empty. Assad's portrait, old posters, and graffiti were plastered all over the metal shutters. Uncle Najim's family and Grandmother Maryam took the second-floor apartment, ours took the third, and Uncle Mohammed's would eventually occupy the top floor. The neighbourhood, Sayyidah Zaynab, was a rough place and its people were gruff, uneducated, and staunchly religious. We hated the place, but the rent was cheap and there were hardly any police or soldiers around. All the men searched for work, but it was scarce. Eventually, Naser and Abdullah landed jobs in a bakery, with bare-bones pay and long hours. Uncle Najim was so preoccupied with finding work that we weren't even enrolled in school. There wasn't much point anyway because most of the schools were routinely closed for safety reasons. That much, I was happy about. But soon, without the distraction of school, life became monotonous.

Without the burden of school or the joy of helping Father at the bakery, my day became a cycle of chores, *Counter-Strike*, cousins. There was very little else to do. Eventually, we took to hanging out on the rooftop of our building. We'd bring up steaming cups of tea and just stare at Damascus below, numb with boredom.

One lazy morning, we were sipping our tea, backs bent like old men, when Ali came bursting up the rooftop stairs with a clear plastic rice sack.

"Look, guys! We can make a kite!" he crowed.

Yousef, Aziz, and I looked at each other and burst into laughter. When we were Alush's age, we had loved flying kites.

"Kites, Ali? What are we, five? Dude!" We could barely catch our breath, we were snickering so hard.

Ali glared hard at us, his lip curled. "*Inchibb!* Shut up! Fine," he sputtered, "but do you geniuses have anything else for us to do?"

He had us. We looked at each other. We looked at the sad little sack.

Aziz sighed. "We'll need sticks to make the frame."

Yousef, the oldest, gave into his boredom. "And string . . ."

"Well . . . *aiwa*, we could fight them. Remember that? Our kite fights?"

Ali whooped, pumping his fists and tossing the bag in the air. "Yeah! This will be great, you'll see!" He threw punches at us, high-kicking the air. "Fighter kites, hwah!" We laughed.

Funnily enough, Ali was right. It *was* great. That stupid kite project preoccupied us for nearly two months. It had been a long time since any of us had made a kite, and our first few careened and crashed on their maiden flights. We scavenged for whatever materials we could find but because it felt so silly and childish, we didn't tell anyone else about our project. Mother and my aunties would giggle at us as they drank their coffees together. We thought we were being so sneaky, but they knew what we were up to. Once, I think Mother purposefully left out an old rice bag for me to find. We hunted for thin wooden dowels and branches for the frames. Any kind of scrap plastic. Kitchen string, fishing twine, discarded flyers for the paper chain kite tails to keep the kites flying high and stable.

In the end, we each made a high-flying, somewhat shabby-looking kite. They sailed from our rooftop out over crowded, cramped, coarse Damascus. The brisk breezes that brought the smell of jasmine flowers carried our kites high. For those moments, we forgot everything we were trying to escape. We would wrap our fingers with tape or toilet paper to prevent the string from cutting into our fingers. Each dance and jerk of the hands caused the kite to flit about. There was magic in that; we had absolute control over this one thing. Four boys, four kites, our laughter and those kite tails whipping in the wind.

Once we were confident about our kites' abilities, we started fighting them. Seeing your own kite dip and dive in the sky wasn't enough. You'd see your cousin's kite dancing in the breeze and you'd just have to take it down. We didn't have the means or expertise to coat our kite strings in glass fragments like the real traditional kite fighters did; instead, we just tried to knock the other kites down, without sacrificing our own. One by one, our kites fell. First Ali's, then mine. Finally, it was just Aziz and Yousef. Their kites ended up so hopelessly tangled that we were in danger of losing both. As each boy tried to wrest control over his kite, frustration brought out the elbows, and they jostled at each other as they tried to untangle the strings. Curses rained down.

"Ahh, gimme that!" I yelped as I grabbed the string out of Yousef's hand. At that exact moment, both strings snapped and the two kites went crashing into the street below, careening into someone's laundry line, dresses flapping in the wind. Peals of laughter.

"Ugh, so much for that," grumbled Ali.

IF IT WAS POSSIBLE, Damascus brought my cousins and me even closer together. Back in Homs, we'd had our separate schools and soccer teams, but in Damascus, we only had each other. Every few mornings, I would visit the Bank of Father and he'd drop a few coins in my hand. We were living off our small savings and a meagre stipend from the UN agency, but Father understood the necessity of having us occupied.

Another lazy afternoon in the arcade: the foosball table was busy so we gave ourselves over to *Counter-Strike*. Yousef, Aziz, Abdullah and I were just starting to lose ourselves in play when the clatter of metal shutters pierced our concentration. Everyone in the arcade looked up, straining to see in the dim room, the only light coming from the arcade games and pop machine at the back. The wide-eyed owner mouthed, "*Shabiha*," and

waved everyone into the back corner. He gestured
and mimed wildly for us all to crouch or sit down.
Everyone obliged as the world rumbled outside.
My gut cramped in pain and fear. Hiding here
in the dark felt more dangerous, somehow, and I
couldn't stand it. I stood up. I shook my head at
my cousins and the storeowner shot a murderous
look at me. "Sit. Down. Little boy!"

I don't know if it was because I couldn't see
what was going on outside, or not being given
a choice in how to act, being chided like a child,
or being away from my family. Every fibre of
my being was just telling me to get out of there.
"I'm sorry, sir. I know you're trying to help us but
I can't . . . I have to go to my family." I whispered
evenly.

Silence. Rather than risk an outburst with me, he
led me to the back exit. A furtive glance to the left
and right then I bolted into the sunlight, zigzagging
down the alley. Then, footsteps pounded behind
me, spurring me to go faster. Suddenly, hands
grasped my shoulders and I was yanked backwards.

"Idiot! Don't do that! Don't take off on your own.
We do this together. If the shabiha takes you, they
will have to take us together."

My cousins stared hard at me and I saw myself
reflected in their faces. They were right. Together.

Through everything, we were more than cousins —
we were brothers.

I nodded and Abdullah led the way home.

IN THE END, we only stayed in Damascus
for about six months. Right around my twelfth
birthday in March, Father started wondering out
loud if we shouldn't just return to Homs. The
rumours said that things had quieted down back
there, but here in Damascus there was more
violence in the streets. In particular, the people of
Sayyidah Zaynab felt more dangerous. There was
more than one religious zealot around. Worse yet,
there were those who claimed to be religious but
were only pledged to violence. Many men carried
concealed knives, keeping with the old traditions.
Danger lurked in plain clothes and in uniforms.

Financially, we were struggling. None of the
adults could hold onto a steady job so even they
paced around like caged animals, just like the kids.
My father and uncles took turns going down to
the UN agency to check on our applications and
whenever they returned, they shook their heads
and went out on long walks together to talk away
from our ears. On the issue of moving, there was
a break in the ranks. My uncles disagreed with

Father about returning to Homs. And, as much as we hated it in Damascus, my sisters and I wanted to stay near our cousins. Mother seemed ambivalent and resigned. During one of our many family dinners together, Uncle Najim turned to Father in frustration, "Hafedh, we need to do this together." The tension between the adults was rising and they were at a strange stalemate I couldn't understand.

A week later, Father and Naser returned to Homs on a reconnaissance trip. They wanted to see for themselves what it was like back home. They found the atmosphere was more relaxed and there were far fewer soldiers and police in the streets. Many old checkpoints appeared abandoned and the neighbourhood felt much emptier. We weren't the only ones who had fled Homs.

A month after my birthday, we moved back. A few weeks later, Uncle Najim and then Uncle Mohammed moved back as well. The strange, silent tension settled. There was nothing for us in Damascus, we were all home. Together.

9

Oh, Father

And so, life continued and it even got brighter.
We returned to school for the final few months of
the school year and I found myself back in Grade
Six. Abdil Aziz enrolled in a collegiate institution,
his dreams set on university and maybe even
law school. Father reopened Baserah Bakery and
installed a sunny yellow awning in the front.

A few blocks away from our apartment building,
there was an abandoned construction site with
the concrete shell of a building at the far end of
an empty field. The tall building was meant to

be the corporate office of a car company, and its main floor was going to be a shiny new dealership. The wide parking lot in front was supposed to be for all the new cars parked out front, waiting for customers. Construction halted a few months after it began because there was so much bombing in the area. This was the perfect spot for our massive soccer games. We would call or text all our friends and descend on the field. Some of us would try to show off and do tricks. Gaggles of teenagers would hang out and watch all the action. It was a place where we could just relax and be normal.

One afternoon, Amro and I threaded the maze of alleys on our way to the field, jostling and bouncing my soccer ball between us. The chain-link fenced loomed in front of us but as we neared, it was too quiet. We stopped in our tracks. Instinct kicked in, and we scooted behind a stone wall, listening hard, scanning the deserted construction site. *Where is everybody*, our raised eyebrows asked.

A short, low whistle of scheming kids. Our heads pivoted towards the sound, and there, we saw our friend Ali and a bunch of other boys crouched behind an old dumpster facing the field, two streets over. Ali pulled out his phone and started texting: "My dad thinks the army have set up in the building."

"*Inchibb*. Seriously? What would the army want with an abandoned construction site, anyway?"

Ali glanced right, then left, then dashed from his hiding spot to us. He left a telling trail of dust as he ran.

"Al Shammas." Ali nodded in the direction behind the building. "The army is always pounding the rebels living there. From that height, they have a perfect shot into that neighbourhood."

The rumble of an army SUV sent us crouching back behind the wall. An officer with a mean-looking rifle slung over his back jumped out of the back of the old Jeep and he unlocked the giant padlock that now secured the chain-link gate. Until today, the gate was never locked. The Jeep drove through the gate and waited while the officer locked up and jumped back in. It peeled away towards the building.

Amro and I looked at each other, confused and curious. Ali was pointing wildly at his own back then at the soldier's. "Dragunov!" he breathed, nodding knowingly. We all knew that name from *Counter-Strike*. Dragunov, the sniper rifle: that was what the soldier was carrying. My heart sank. One more thing the stupid war stole from us. Here, where we spent so many afternoons playing soccer, the army was building a sniper's nest.

AS MORE PEOPLE trickled back into Homs, business was picking up in Baserah Bakery, and I was needed more days of the week. After school finished at noon, I'd show up at the bakery around two and help out until we closed at seven.

One late afternoon, I was carrying a twenty-five pound bag of salt to the bakery when I stumbled in the street and fell. I landed on a bunch of rubble but I didn't cut myself or anything, so I just brushed off the sharp pain. Later that night, I woke up drenched in sweat and my insides were boiling. By morning, I had barely slept and was so drained that I couldn't even tell Mother what was wrong. A day of rest was prescribed for me by Father, but by the following morning, I was so weak from the shooting pains, I was taken directly to the hospital.

In Syria, there were public and private health-care systems. Although the public hospitals did not inspire a lot of confidence, we had no choice since we couldn't afford a private one. Everything looked old and dingy and it took hours to even be examined. When the doctor finally appeared, he poked me briefly in the abdomen, ordered blood tests, and was gone in a matter of minutes. More waiting. In the bed next to mine, there was a despondent girl, about my age. She moaned constantly in her sleep and her eye bulged, frightfully, from her eye socket.

The entire right side of her face looked collapsed, a blotchy mess of purple stains. The girl scared me more than my pain. I didn't know how long she had been lying there. There were no bandages on her face. What would happen to me?

Six hours crawled by with my mother and sisters doing their best to distract me as I drifted in and out of sleep. The doctor suddenly reappeared with the diagnosis: appendicitis. He explained that my appendix could burst at any moment and that I would need to undergo surgery as soon as possible. No food or water before the surgery.

Then he left and didn't return for another twelve hours. I blubbered through the sharp pains. At one point, a tired-looking nurse came in to give me an IV. As she fumbled listlessly with the needle, I looked down at my arm, and blood spurted from my vein after her third failed attempt at insertion. I couldn't even turn away from the grisly sight. And in that torturous time, it wasn't just my appendix but also my stomach that cramped in pain. In hunger. It's not like I wasn't used to fasting. During Ramadan, we go without food or water for ten or more hours every day. I could bear that. But I couldn't bear Father.

Sometime later in the evening after Mother

took my sisters home, Father came strolling up to my hospital bed.

"Oh, my son. Abu Bakr, such a life we have." He sighed and plunked himself in the chair beside my bed. I turned feebly towards him. A rustle of wrappers and the intoxicating warm smell of roast beef. My mouth watered, viciously.

His eyes positively danced with mischief. My drooling mouth dropped in disbelief as he took a hearty bite of his shawarma. Pillowy soft, slightly charred pita embraced a mess of juicy, spit-roasted beef. Lettuce, cucumbers, tomatoes. The meat juices mingled with the cool yogurty sauce and ran down Father's hands as he bit down again, greedily.

I stared.

"Hungry, son?" He couldn't help himself, laughter choked him. Little bits of pita flew out of his mouth.

I couldn't help it, I cried. This only spurred his laughter more.

"Oh son, you're hungry? Oh, so it can't be that bad. See, Bakr? You're not dying. You'll be fine!" Love radiated from him, but all I wanted was that shawarma. Oh, Father. This is how we passed the last few hours before my surgery, Father teasing me, making jokes, and reliving old stories. I drifted in and out of sleep, the pain temporarily forgotten.

After the surgery, I stayed in the hospital for a week, recovering. My many visitors brought me bags of my favourite candy and Grandmother made her *warak enab*, grape leaves stuffed with rice and beef, especially for me. Father was there nearly the whole time. At the end of my ordeal in the hospital, the only thing I really lost was my chubby cheeks.

10

The Night of Power

During Ramadan, our lives were turned upside down, but in a good way. Our whole daily routine flipped. We fasted from sunrise to sunset, so we slept during the day and stayed awake through the night. In this time, we were supposed to empty ourselves of all the little things that preoccupied our daily lives and redirect our hearts towards worship. And, by not eating or even drinking water, we were supposed to be reminded of the suffering of the less fortunate and develop more empathy for others. We emptied ourselves of immoral thoughts and bad behavior; we refocused on devotion and charity.

The streets were strung up with glowing crescent moons, twinkling lights, and colourful lanterns, and since everyone stayed up all night, the streets felt like a huge block party. We would all sleep from four in the morning until three in the afternoon. There would be prayers in the early evening until the sun went down and when night arrived, we would break the fast together with *iftar*, which always began with three sticky dates, a sweet yogurt drink, and hearty lentil soup. When we returned home after mosque, we would enjoy a lively meal of lamb, kebabs, vegetables, and rice, and always sweet black tea. After that, we would just hang out, snacking, playing games, and watching TV and movies. There were often Ramadan TV specials. Even though Grandmother used to nag us for watching too much TV throughout the year, she would join us to watch movies during Ramadan. For that month, life took on a different rhythm.

However, the Ramadan before I began Grade Seven turned my life upside down in a different way. On the twenty-third day of Ramadan, August 1, 2013, a part of me emptied out in a way I'll never fully be able to fill again. The twenty-third night is known as one of the nights of power. That day, I witnessed an unholy, terrifying power.

It was mid-afternoon when we were woken by the explosions. Aunt Ateka, Aziz, and his sister Dilal had stayed the night. Aziz, Alush, and I were snoring in my bedroom and we all jolted up at once. By this time, we were mostly used to the sounds of bomb blasts, but these ones shook the house — they must have been nearby. The whistle and shudder of mortars. Bottom lip jutting out, Alush quietly slipped under Aziz's blanket and nuzzled into him as we listened intently. Silence, then shuffles in the other rooms. I tiptoed slowly down the hall to see Father at the front windows already. He stared hard outside, neck straining. Another explosion, a little further off. When I joined him, he hesitated then quietly said, "Son, get everyone up and ready to go, okay?"

I knocked on my sisters' and Mother's doors. "Let's go! Come on! Up, up!" I called in an even voice.

There was a rush of activity and running water. Mother, Aunt Ateka, and Maryam began pulling out the drinks and dates for iftar but Father called to them, "No time for that!" Although the explosions didn't sound any closer, the intensity of the bombing continued. That familiar itch in my feet returned and my stomach was all in knots, not from the hunger but from the sight of Father, tensely on watch at the window. Father shook his head and then turned to us.

"*Bismillah*, our documents. Let's go!"

Some of us weren't even dressed yet. Alush stood half-asleep in his blue Ninja Turtles pyjamas while the women hastily tossed on their hijab head coverings. I scooped up Alush and he gripped me tightly, burying his face in my neck. We barrelled out of the apartment with Father in the lead and Mother a step behind him. Aunt Ateka and Abeer had a death-grip on each other as we ran down the street. Where were we running? Where do you go when you don't even know where the danger is coming from?

Heavy traffic on Sham Avenue finally stopped our panicked flight. We were only a few blocks from our building. Father started counting us. "Abrar? Abrar!"

"Hey! Heeyyyyyyy!" We all turned at the sound of Abrar's bewildered voice and saw her stomping towards us in her pink Barbie pyjamas. She clumsily dragged Aunt Ateka's overstuffed bag behind her, famous Abrar scowl on her face, furious at being left behind. We huddled around her, apologizing profusely under the trees of the busy boulevard while we waited for the street-lights to change. We were all panting. Father bent over, hands on his knees, catching his breath. Aziz frantically texted Uncle Mohammed. Aunt Ateka and my sisters giggled at how Auntie had run out wearing a pair of men's flip-flops while clutching her own shoes in the other hand.

As I set Alush on his feet gently, I smiled at him. "It's okay, Alush. I'll race you, okay?" I ruffled his hair and he looked up at me, uncertainly. He put his small hand in mine.

Suddenly, the deadly crackle and thunder of Grad rockets, and a vicious shaking. I tugged Alush behind me, and my jaw dropped. Maybe a few hundred metres away, a monstrous fireball swallowed the sky. The sound of shattering windows echoed all around as a brutal wave of heat blew past us. Pitch-black smoke and hellfire mushroomed hundreds of metres into the sky, and in that moment I was certain we would all die. It wasn't a shaky, hiccupping fear. It was simply a chilling certainty that settled into my bones and drained me of all feeling.

"Ya Allah," Aziz gasped beside me, "Oh my God."

For a brief moment, even the army was stunned silent. Then all around us people screamed in terror and shouted, "*Allah akbar.*" God must be greater than this evil. Behind us, Abeer let out an animal shriek. My whole family turned and looked at her, in shock at the primal sound that came from the quietest of us.

I stood there, frozen. Father tapped my shoulder.

"Let's go, Bakr! Uncle Najim's!"

It took my brain a few beats to process what was going on, but we were running again. Since the rest of his family was visiting relatives in Iraq, Uncle Najim was home alone and Naser had gone to stay overnight with him. We were only a few blocks away and soon, we were huffing up the stairs of Uncle Najim's building. Inside, we found Naser sleeping, of all things! "How could you sleep through that?" I kicked him awake. I didn't know anyone who could sleep as deeply as my brother. In the living room, Mother silently cried because Uncle Najim wasn't there. He must have been at mosque for prayers already and we knew his mosque was close to where that fireball had roared to life. No one knew what to do and we all looked at my father. "Mohammed's. Let's go." With that, we were all up on our feet again.

Back out on the street, Father started shouting and waving his arms wildly. A white Suzuki open-back micro van screeched to a stop; Father knew the driver well. He hopped into the tiny front cab and we piled into the back, all thirteen of us. We squeezed onto each other's laps with Alush lying down across our knees but none of this really registered. I only saw the fury of smoke and fire in the sky. The sight of that fireball left me cold, and I shivered despite the searing heat of August and the bodies I was pressed against.

Ten cramped minutes later, we raced up the flights of steps to Uncle Mohammed's apartment. For the rest of the evening, no one could speak of anything else. Prayers and meals came and went but I was numb to it all. The evening news described it as a rocket attack on a weapons depot but I still couldn't process anything other than the sound of all those windows shattering at once. Everyone teased Abeer about her scream. Keeping with Ramadan traditions, all the women wore black hijabs and *abayas*, so my sisters laughed about how they must've looked like a propaganda ad for ISIS in the back of that moving van. Only thing missing was the donkey. There my family was, out on the balcony, joking amongst the potted geraniums and eating dessert like nothing had happened. But it did happen. Sometimes, to convince myself, I watch and rewatch a video of that explosion on YouTube. And the crazy thing is, that night, even though it was one of the holiest nights of Ramadan, all the mosques were silent and dark. No one dared venture out. The streets were abandoned. No joyous *iftar* banquets. No *muezzins* climbing their minarets to sing their stirring calls to prayer.

Around eight that evening, Father, Naser, and Mother rose off the couch. Father waved me over to the front door. As I approached them, his eyes met mine squarely and he pressed a bundle into my hands. He nodded firmly and cupped my right cheek.

"I'm going to go check on the house and Naser will check on the bakery. You stay with the family, OK?"

In my hands were all our documents and a bundle of cash. The door closed softly as I realized what this package meant. I stared at the closed door. I felt my mother's warm hand on my elbow, turning me back towards the loud living room.

"Come, Bakr."

For the rest of the evening, my cousins chatted and laughed above me but I was sinking into my fear. I wished Father was in the apartment with us. I wished Naser was here, my naggy-take-charge-I'm-the-boss big brother. No matter the situation or what he said, his voice sounded like there was laughter in it. I wanted that bundle to be in his hands, instead of mine. I wished none of this had ever happened to us. I tried to lose myself in the noise but I couldn't stand the chatter and cajoling so I just pretended to watch TV. Thankfully, morning approached and everything quieted down. Prayers, a quick meal, then everyone retired to the bedrooms. I was wide awake on the floor of Aziz, Yousef, and Ibrahim's bedroom, with that bundle of cash and documents as my pillow. Alush was curled into me, snoring softly, like a puppy.

Since coming to Syria, I had experienced two shootings at my mosque, witnessed two massacres, and my school had been destroyed. Still, at no point in those three years did I ever once think I would die. Until that day, at the sight of that fireball. Why would Allah will it? Why would a loving God ever allow this kind of violence to happen to anyone? Was it God's plan for children to suffer? For people to die in the streets, murdered? I loved my God, my religion. But, sometimes, deep in that place where my fear hides, I couldn't understand why I had to live like this. How could the God of my gentle father be the same God of those crazy fanatics who killed in the name of Islam? I hated those people the most. How could they take something so loving and peaceful and twist it to justify violence and murder? Those people cannot really be Muslim because my God was about love, peace, charity.

That whole night, I prayed for answers. I prayed for Father and Naser. I prayed for my family. I prayed for peace, not from the war, but peace in my heart.

At last, it was six in the morning and the phone rang. I sat straight up and bolted out into the hallway. Uncle Mohammed opened his bedroom door, on the phone already. He nodded and grinned at me, relief plain as day on his face. It was Father. I murmured a deep prayer of gratitude, stumbled back to the bedroom, and collapsed onto my blanket. I fell asleep instantly.

Later that morning, we walked home together and Alush excitedly pointed out some newly bombed-out buildings. The crumbling buildings depressed me the most. This beautiful city, with its wide, tree-lined boulevards, tall white buildings, and bustling streets had turned into a bombed-out scene from *Counter-Strike*. Instead of balconies lined with colourful carpets being aired out or bright lines of laundry drying in the sun, buildings were cracked and hollowed out. Where there were once billboards of movie stars and neon signs for barbers, restaurants, and computer stores, there

were now bullet-ridden, caved-in walls. Gone were
the little parks where you could lie on the grass,
basking in the sun. In their place, massive piles
of broken concrete and twisted rebar gashed the
ground. My sisters clucked on about some movie.
Father had already bumped into us on the street
earlier, his arms full with grocery bags. My cell
vibrated in my pocket and I fished it out. A text
from Amro: "Soccer? Akrama school field." Why not?

FEBRUARY 2014
Winter

Four months after the terror of that explosion at
the weapons depot, a very odd thing happened: a
vicious winter storm swept through most of Syria
and the Middle East. One December morning,
I woke up to see our birdcages and chicken coops
covered in inches of snow. Of course, snow
during the winter months in Syria was not totally
unheard of, but it normally melted within hours of
falling. This year, the snow just kept falling. I ran
outside to bring my birds in and I was surprised at
how quiet the world was. The bombed-out shells

of buildings were blanketed by snow, the buzz of Homs muffled and silent. It was almost beautiful.

After the snow finally melted, the last winter months remained bitterly cold. On the morning of February 9, Grandmother phoned me in a panic. Soldiers were raiding their apartment building, looking for weapons or suspected rebels. The sounds of boots kicking open doors and muffled shouts drifted up to the top floor. Her voice was barely a whisper. "Please, Abu Bakr, come get me."

When I arrived, I waited around the corner to make sure the army had moved on to the next building. No sounds. No *shabiha*. I sprinted up the stairs and had barely tapped at the door when it swung open and there she was, trembling, eyes glazed. Her clammy hand gripped mine. "*Alhamdulillah*, Abu Bakr, praise God you're here . . ."

I took her by her shoulders as gently as I could but I was shocked by how tiny she felt next to me; my grandmother had never felt small before. She was pale and kept stumbling and I couldn't wrap my mind around how changed she was. Just last week, she had been kicking our feet off the couch and nagging us to help her start cleaning up the garden in preparation for spring. Now as we shuffled home together, we had to stop for little breaks every block so that she could catch her breath, even though she never seemed to be able to.

When we finally got to our apartment, Abeer and Mother rushed out to greet her. Mother's eyes widened with worry, just for a flash. Those short moments of the army raid left my grandmother a hollow shell of who she used to be.

I settled Grandmother onto the couch with a blanket while Abeer brought her a bowl of lentil soup. Blankly, Grandmother stared at it for a long time before she finally waved it away. Abrar bounced in with an orange and a paring knife; she loved to watch the way Grandmother could peel the entire orange in one long, winding strip. "No, little one, I'm not hungry. My stomach hurts," Grandmother whispered. She barely spoke a word after that, other than mumbled prayers.

That's what terror does to you. It weakens you. It deflates you, as it did my grandmother. We hovered around her for the rest of the day and it was decided that she would stay at our place until she recovered her strength.

Later that night, Grandmother Maryam died quietly in her sleep, nestled amongst my sleeping sisters.

TWO MONTHS AFTER my grandmother passed, that car bomb went off outside our apartment and I buried a man's jawbone. The crinkling sound of the white plastic bag and the dirt and gravel hitting it lingered. Not knowing what else to do, I buried myself in work, just like Grandmother used to. As soon as school was finished for the day, I would grab a quick lunch on my way to the bakery. I had convinced Father and Abdil Karim to teach me how to start the dough for the bakers to form, but while I was kneading it, folding it over and over, images of the stones over Grandmother's shrouded body rose in my mind. Friends dropped by, pockets jingling with coins for the arcade, but I just waved them away. Amro showed up juggling a soccer ball on his foot, challenging me to a game, but I just disappeared to the back with a mumbled excuse.

When the spring sun finally started to take the chill off that brutal winter, Father got the idea to plant rose bushes in the bakery's courtyard because they reminded him of his grandfather's farm back in Iraq. He said we needed to make things beautiful again. Standing in the peaceful space with the new rose bushes, it dawned on me to start selling drinks so that our customers could sit and enjoy them. Business was bustling at the Baserah Bakery, its cheerful awning a beacon for our customers. Our chewy flatbread was different from the typical thin, hollow Syrian pita that people got from the government bakeries. Father even had to hire three more employees, and they were all like uncles to me.

My drink stand enterprise started with a foam cooler box filled with ice and bottles of pop and juice. Father allowed me to sell the cold drinks in our courtyard, where we had set up a few café tables and chairs. I was in charge of all the cash flow and stock; Father allowed me to keep the earnings. I even convinced him to buy a small fridge. We shook hands over a deal for my drinks to be sold even when I wasn't working in the bakery.

I loved it all. I felt like I was a business partner with my father and longed to be at the bakery instead of at school. The only thing I enjoyed about school was gym class. Our classes were getting more and more crowded because so many schools had been destroyed. Many teachers had fled, or been killed. Worse yet, school meant I was away from my family. Ever since the car bomb exploded steps from home, whenever I heard explosions or fighter jets, my feet itched to take me home. I had terrible visions of finding the jawbone, not of a stranger, but of my family. When this happened, it felt like the world went into fast-forward mode.

Everything sped up – my thoughts, my fears – and I'd mindlessly rush through whatever assignment I happened to be working on, hand it in to the teacher, race to the office, and ask for permission to go home. The principal was a kind woman. She saw that my fear was genuine and always allowed me to go. I'd race home and as soon as I was there, my heart would settle. My sisters and cousins were relentless in their taunts, pointing out that even Alush, now in Grade Two, was brave enough to stay at school, but I couldn't help it. At first, Father tried to understand, but after a while, even he prodded me to stay at school. Only Mother was sympathetic, but then again, I think she would have preferred to keep us all closer to her. Her worry made her age before our eyes. Near the beginning of the civil war, during one particularly bad night of shelling, Father had said we would live together and die together, and I guess that's why I wanted to always be near someone in my family. I didn't want to die away from them.

All the events that had happened since we arrived in Syria had changed me in many ways, but after that jawbone, I wanted to *choose* to change myself. I wanted to be harder, tougher, like those cold, unsmiling people in Damascus. I had assumed that they were just unfriendly, but now I wondered if they closed themselves off to protect themselves. Maybe if you didn't care, you couldn't be hurt.

The sad truth was, you could not live in Syria and have a clean heart. How could you, when you live in a place where you're randomly shot at and car bombs explode outside your home? I wanted my heart to be pure, but already I hated people and I hated parts of my life. Sometimes, I even hated my family. I questioned my faith and my religion. I questioned my father. Sometimes, I was so angry that I just wanted to hit someone, anyone. No, my heart was not clean. So, if it wasn't clean, why shouldn't I be cold and tough? I wanted to stop being Abu Bakr: happy, big cheeks, smiling Abu Bakr. I wanted to be tough, so tough that no one could ever hurt me.

Truthfully, I tried. I tried to be hard and uncaring by ignoring my friends or shutting my family out. But as soon as I was with Father or my uncles, my old self took over. I couldn't help it: it was just the way Father teased me, or joked with my sisters. The way his eyes would search for mine in a crowded street when we were out buying supplies for the bakery. He always pulled me back to myself somehow. I watched Father a lot. He was neither hard nor soft. He was both, silently strong.

He loved people, but he also protected us fiercely. I wanted, so much, to be just like my father. In the end, my tough veneer faded away.

And then, out of nowhere, we got some relief. At the end of April, Naser delivered the good news: our refugee application was back in progress and the five adults would have to go to Damascus for their second security-screening interview with our newly assigned visa officer.

12

Thirteen

The relief was short-lived. One night in May, my
phone trilled at 11:30 p.m. Calls that late made my
stomach drop and I lunged at my phone at the first
ring. It was my cousin Haneen, and all she said, in
a panicked hiss, was, "Come." I jumped up off the
couch and ran outside to find Naser, sneaking a
cigarette in the garden.

"Naser! Uncle Najim! I don't know what's
happened but Haneen just called and hung up."

He stomped out his cigarette. "Get Father. Let's go."

I ran inside to find Father and tried to knock without waking my sisters in the next room. I think, by then, we were always alert, even in our sleep, because I barely finished knocking when Father yanked open the door. "What happened?"

As I told him, I could see the colour drain from my mother's lips. "Go," she gasped.

I don't remember much of the mad dash to Uncle Najim's apartment. I could hear my father's uneven breath as we ran. Naser kept trying to call his friends for help, struggling to keep up with us. I hadn't been out in the streets that late in years, thanks to Father's curfew, so I was actually scared at how empty and dark the streets were. There were no sounds except our footsteps echoing dangerously. My teeth chattered so loudly that I thought it would bring the *shabiha* running.

"Wait," Father waved us to slow down, "wait, quiet, listen first." We were just around the corner from Najim's building and we all stopped to listen, our hearts pounding in our throats. No sounds, no *shabiha*. Naser peered round the corner and waved us on. Inside, we found my aunt clutching onto Haneen, Ali staring blankly out the window, and three little girls sobbing uncontrollably.

"Ya Allah, what happened?" Father asked quietly.

"They hit him, Uncle! Oh my God! They punched him until he fell to the ground! Then Abdullah! They kicked him so hard! Oh my God, oh my God!" Raiyan, her gigantic eyes swimming in tears, could barely speak in between her sobs. Naser ran out to the hallway dialing more numbers while Haneen told us what had happened before we arrived.

Only half an hour earlier, Uncle Najim and Haneen were roused from sleep by the sound of voices in the street below. Peering through the window together, they saw Abdullah arguing with a friend in front of a parked car. Suddenly, a sharp whistle pierced the night and Abdullah bolted into the apartment building while his friend dashed off down the street. Uncle Najim bounded for the bedroom while Haneen ran to yank open the front door for her older brother. Abdullah charged up the steps and slammed the door behind him. With wild eyes and fumbling hands, he pulled the battery off his cellphone and thrust the whole thing at his sister: "Hide this. They're coming." He ducked into the bathroom. Haneen heard the snap of a plastic SIM card and the flush of a toilet and then they all heard the thundering of combat boots.

Uncle Najim, document papers in hand, came out just as the officers burst into the apartment. Haneen slipped into her bedroom and got under the covers next to Raiyan, whose whole body was stiff with horror. "Shh, pretend you're sleeping. Shh," Haneen breathed. She groped for her own cellphone, hastily dialled a number and panted, "Come," then quietly snapped her phone shut and drew the blankets around herself and her little sisters.

All four girls huddled closer together and pretended to squeeze their eyes shut while Ali, blissfully unaware, continued to snore in his own corner of the room. Their bedroom door was open just wide enough for Raiyan to peak and see everything happening in the living room from where she lay.

"Father told the police," Raiyan sobbed. "He said 'He's a good son! I don't know his friends, but my Abdullah, he's a good son! Take me! Whatever it is, blame me, take me!' But they didn't listen, Uncle! They dragged Abdullah out of the bathroom. Father tried to show them his ID papers and they just laughed at him. Ya Allah! And Mother! She . . . she was so smart! She saw one of the soldiers hide Father's papers in his pocket! Mother, she said, 'I saw you hide my husband's papers! Just look, sir! Please!' And then they hit Father so hard, Uncle! Oh my god!"

"It was Abdullah's friend's fault. You know, The Sheikh." Haneen took Raiyan by her shoulders and rubbed her back. I didn't know The Sheikh, but I had heard about him through whispers amongst my friends. The rumour was, Abdullah's old friend was now heavily involved with Thuwar, an anti-government and anti-isis group.

"They took them, Uncle. They took Father and Abdullah!" Raiyan broke down.

That night was a blur. Father, Naser, and I tried to call everyone we could think of who could help. Most people didn't answer their phones. Others hung up as soon as we mentioned that Uncle and Abdullah had been taken. Sometime early in the morning, Father sent me to bed with my cousins and ordered us to get some sleep.

When I woke up after a few fitful hours, Naser had gone out to track down a friend who worked in the government. Through him, we found out that Uncle Najim, Abdullah, and The Sheikh had been arrested that night. The adults huddled in the kitchen to talk and I heard *bribe* muttered many times. Abdullah's friends kept dropping by throughout the day, heads bowed and murmuring apologies to my aunt Muna.

I sat at the edge of those conversations, trying to understand. But also, I sat watching Raiyan, Maram, and Islam cry quietly over their colouring books and uneaten lunches. I didn't know if I was angry, determined, or sad, but I was glad Grandmother wasn't with us anymore. Witnessing that scene would have broken her heart, for sure.

It was two days before Uncle Najim and Abdullah returned. It wasn't the bruises, the perfectly round cigarette burns, or the split lips that shocked me. It was Uncle Najim's hair. His jet-black hair was suddenly streaked with grey.

Weeks later, when I got up the courage to ask him if it hurt to be beaten up, he sat thinking for a long time. Finally, he looked me square in the eyes and he said, "No, little one, it didn't hurt, *Alhamdulillah*. When those men hit you, your mind goes somewhere else. You only think of your family and you don't feel the pain. You just see those beautiful faces."

AFTER LOSING GRANDMOTHER and nearly losing Abdullah and Uncle Najim, I lost interest in everything for a while, even the bakery and my drink stand. School was even more unbearable than usual. The bright spring skies beckoned to me, and I didn't want to sleep through another English class.

One particularly warm morning, I was steps from the school when I was assaulted from behind by a barrage of slaps and shoves. Ali and Amro tried to tackle me to the ground and we tussled in the sunlight, laughing and shouting insults at each other until the bell pierced through our laughter.

Amro heaved a great sigh and bent over to scoop up his cap and books. Another morning of drudgery in the classroom. The three of us hustled to join our class line-up in the school's courtyard for the daily singing of the Syrian national anthem. We stood, stone-faced, through the music. As the students trudged towards first period, I grabbed Amro by the elbow and yanked him around a corner.

"Dude! You're going to make me late! Let go, Bakr!"

"Ah! Screw it! Let's go, *aiwa!*" Mischief, absolute mischief.

We snickered quietly in agreement: we would skip. We hid in the hall until all sound had died down then we made a run for it. Freedom! We spent a glorious morning in the park, a few blocks from school. While sharing a few bottles of soda, we hung out and played soccer. The next morning, another escape, but this time Ali also joined us, in the arcade playing foosball. Skipping soon became a habit. We didn't get caught at first because it wasn't unusual for students not to show up for a few days. There was a civil war happening, after all, and we were smart enough not to do it every day. Other kids caught onto our game much sooner than the teachers did, so there were packs of teenagers hanging out in the park most mornings.

For the next few weeks, we continued our game uninterrupted until a few teachers showed up at the park. Shouts rang out and a bunch of kids started running out of the park, laughing and screeching their heads off. The whole herd turned, spotted the danger, and scattered like antelope. The teachers gave chase, madly waving their arms, yelling out commands. Ali, Amro, and I managed to escape capture and once we were safely hidden in the alley, we doubled over in laughter. The crack-up turned to snorts and shrieks, to wheezing and tears. It felt unimaginably good to be belly-laughing like that with Ali and Amro. We staggered to school, giggles erupting every few steps.

Even though I hadn't been physically caught by my teachers that day, Father and my principal both sat me down for some sobering discussions. I knew it was wrong to skip school but it was fun to do something so childish. After everything that happened, it felt so good just to play. But, Father reminded me I was thirteen now; it was time for me to become a man. When he said that, I realized that I had been trying to find something I'd lost after the first shooting at Zawiya mosque. There was no need for me to put my childhood away — it had already disappeared into the ruins of Homs.

So, gritting my teeth, I set out to find my lost schoolbooks. My teachers constantly lectured me because my black scribblers had been abandoned in their classrooms or tucked under some bench or another. When I turned up in her classroom in search of my workbook, my English teacher rolled her eyes at me and threatened me with a fail in her class if I didn't start doing my homework. Casting my eyes down, I apologized. "Sure, sure, Miss. I will try harder, Miss. Inshallah, if Allah allows it."

She laughed and playfully tossed my book in my direction. "Abu Bakr al Rabeeah! Leave Allah out of your homework! That is up to you! Now get to work, young man, and leave God to bigger problems!"

And that's what I did. Remembering how Grandmother used chores to keep her mind busy, I made school my goal in those last few weeks of Grade Seven. Besides, Naser had only completed

Grade Six, and I was determined to beat him, if only by one more year. Because of my appendectomy the previous year, I had skipped the Grade Six final exams, but I wasn't twice lucky. This time around, I sweated bullets that whole time and I don't recall ever studying that much, but finally, summer holiday arrived.

On the last day of school, report cards were distributed and I couldn't bring myself to go and see, so I didn't. Every day, Father would ask if I had gone to get my report card yet and every day, I told him the school was closed. That wasn't a complete lie — I just didn't tell him that I only ever left to go to the school five minutes before it closed. A full week went by until Father turned to me one morning and said, "Ok, Bakr. No more messing around. Go get your report card this morning."

That afternoon, I slunk into the main office. My principal stood there, waiting. Mine was the only report card that remained on the front desk. "Abu Bakr al Rabeeah. Finally, hello." She rolled up a piece of paper and playfully smacked me on the top of my head. I finally brought my eyes up to hers and she laughed. She handed me the rolled up piece of paper: my report card. I gulped hard and unfurled it. Seventy-one percent! I passed the year by one percent!

"Whooo-eeee!" I laughed and jumped in the air.

Shouting my thanks, I raced to the bakery with my report card hidden under my t-shirt. I snuck up behind Father and shouted, "Hi!" scaring my father and triumphantly waving my seventy-one percent in his face and dancing around the hot bakery. He guffawed. He hadn't thought I'd pass either. That was the last ever report card I got in Syria.

13

The Apprentice

Through the bombs and raids and doubts of our four years in Syria, I wasn't the only one in my family who made it a point to change. My older sister Aiesha did too. Months after my Uncle Najim was arrested, the *shabiha* showed up at our house out of the blue. It was right before lunchtime so only Mother, Maryam, Abeer, and Aiesha were at home. Abeer was outside in the garden beating the dust out of one of the rugs when she spotted a group of *shabiha* entering the apartment building through the front entrance. She scrambled inside to warn everyone but before she could say a word, the pounding of rifle butts on the door interrupted her. Maryam raced to the front door, cellphone in hand. "Come home, Father," was all she managed before she hung up and grabbed the door handle. Mother was at the entrance as Maryam eased the door open gently, all the while flattening herself into the triangle between the open door and the wall. She wasn't wearing a hijab so she didn't want to be seen by strangers. Her heart pounded so loudly, she was sure the seven men who strolled into the apartment could hear her hiding behind the door.

A bearded man took a slow pull from his cigarette and greeted my mother casually. "*Marhabaan*, madam."

Eyes lowered, Mother stammered, "*As-salaam 'alaykum.*"

"Where is your husband? Where are your documents?" he snapped, suddenly not so friendly. Mother thrust her papers at him, quivering. She had heard rumours of kidnapped girls and was desperately afraid that they would take my sisters. She prayed they would stay out of sight as another *shabiha* scanned the living room coolly.

"Iraqi? Why are you in Syria? Why not go back to Iraq? Where is your husband? Do you have any sons? Are you Sunni or Shi'a?" The smoking man peppered my mother with questions and she was practically choking on her words when Aiesha burst into the room, hurriedly pulling her hijab on to cover her head.

"Sir! I will answer your questions!" At the sound of her own clear voice, Aiesha looked as surprised as the *shabiha* were. She pulled herself a little bit taller. "My father is on his way home for lunch and will be here any minute."

The smoking man looked down at the documents in his hand and then back at Mother and Aiesha. He jeered, "Why are you so afraid? There is nothing to fear here, we won't hurt you. We protect people."

"Sir, I'm not scared, I'm just out of breath from running to get my hijab on. What are your questions? How can I help?" Aiesha was steady.

The men stayed only fifteen minutes while my sister answered their questions with ease. Mother was silent, Maryam was pressed behind the front door, and Abeer held her breath in the kitchen. Mother said it was like Aiesha had changed herself in those fifteen minutes. She changed from a young, shrinking girl to a calm, assertive woman right before her eyes. Aiesha glowed quietly with pride, waving the compliment away. "I only wanted to help Mother."

Like Aiesha, we all gained skills that we could not have imagined. Knowledge that we never really wanted to know filtered into our lives. Our ears could pick out the differences between mortars, Grad rockets, and car bombs. We could tell the high notes of the metallic smell of fresh blood on the streets from the low reek of a corpse waiting for days to be found in the rubble. When we milled about the crowded *souks*, our eyes narrowed at the sight of a nervous-looking man or woman. We would wonder and then try to push down that suspicion. We became sensitive gazelles, always stopping to scan and listen. It wasn't a conscious choice – it simply became a part of our way of walking and being.

News reports brought words like *barrel bombs* and *gas attacks* into our lives. Barrel bombs were homemade destruction. A container full of motor oil and explosives dropped from the sky, pouring down liquid fire. Gas: chlorine, mustard, sarin. Images of people foaming at the mouth. We watched news reports of these things happen all over Syria, and prayed we would never live through these ourselves. I would half listen and then not. Some weeks, I would do nothing but constantly check my phone for news updates. Other weeks, I would pretend none of it was real.

At the end of the summer, Father pulled me aside and said, "Tell me, son, how do you feel about not returning to school in September?"

I was confused. Some of my friends had stopped going to school because their parents were too afraid to send their kids to school. "Not returning to school? Why? For all of us?"

"No, just you, son. Your sisters and Alush will continue. They are doing well and they enjoy their studies." He paused. "But you . . . maybe it's better if you take this year off and learn the business with me. You can try school again later, but maybe that isn't the best path for you right now."

Through all the skipping, I had never thought about actually quitting school. I did love being in the business with Father.

"Sure, sure, Father."

September came and my older sisters excitedly returned to school. I tried not to think too much about missing out on classes with my friends. Besides, I was proud to be my father's apprentice. At seven in the morning, Father would go to open the bakery and fire up the ovens. Abdil Karim would start the dough and I would arrive around eight to help him press, slap, and toss the little springy dough balls into floury, flat discs. In the beginning, my hands were clumsy, and Abdil Karim

149

would squawk instructions at me. He'd laugh menacingly but then gently show me, again, how to flip the dough just right. He was tough but also so much fun to be around. After a few months, my hands memorized the dance of the bread. We'd joke throughout the morning while I watched him deftly slip the formed dough and bread in and out of the oven. Around nine, Naser would come in and Father would go home for his breakfast. The rest of the morning and early afternoon passed easily with Naser barking orders and the lively hub of customers exchanging neighbourhood gossip or news about attacks and arrests.

October 1, 2014, was a day that started like any other. I had been at the bakery for two hours. The ovens were popping hot, so I decided to take my break in the shaded boulevard across from the bakery. I was leaning back against a tree and sipping my sweet tea when I heard the roll of an explosion, maybe a few blocks away. Through the tall apartment buildings, billowing smoke and distant screams. A second explosion rang out. I sat up and listened, almost sniffing the air to see if danger was near. Nothing. All I could do was sigh, shake my head, and return to my tea.

My tea was half-finished when people started streaming past me. Kids in their blue school uniforms, covered in dust, some smeared with blood. An old woman, her face streaked with tears, clutching onto a bewildered-looking girl about Ibrahim's age. The air was thick with fear, but also with anger, the fury clear on their faces as they ran by. A man about Naser's age slowed down to a walk a few steps from me.

"Excuse me, sir, what happened this time?"

"Children," he sputtered. "Those evil dogs. It was the elementary school, Akrama Almakhzomi school. A car bomb. Then a suicide bomber." He stormed off, continuing to mutter to himself. Thank God, it wasn't Abrar and Alush's school.

Abdil Karim was crossing the street towards me with a bottle of water in his hand. He surveyed the people running by and his eyes met mine in confusion. I told him what I'd heard and he swore under his breath.

"*Ya Allah*. The death of innocents?" He trailed off, his attention turned to his cellphone. Another employee joined us under the tree, trying to reach his family on his phone. We stared blankly at the people hustling by when Naser came strolling out of the bakery looking for us. I stood up and brushed the dirt off my shorts.

"*Y'allah!* Hurry up! Get back to work!" he called from across the street in mock authority. Pausing to allow people past him, he joined us under the trees as his cellphone rang in his hand. "Hello? Hold on a second." A smile crept on his face and I snickered.

"Hey, Naser, is that the girl I saw you with in the café yesterday?"

"Shut up! Father just got back. He wants to talk to you, Bakr. I'm heading out for a bit." He cracked his grin again, cuffed me on the back of my head, and walked off.

Father approached us, practically bouncing, a broad smile on his face. He slid his arm around my shoulders for a few moments before he cleared his throat and waved the other employees away. "Come, Bakr. Let's talk." We turned back towards the trees. "*Alhamdulillah*, Bakr, this morning, I got a phone call from the UN." My forehead furrowed in confusion.

"So, you know that business trip we took to Damascus last week? Well, that wasn't for business. I didn't want to tell you or your sisters in case it turned out to be nothing, but we actually went to Damascus to visit the Canadian consulate."

"What? Father, I thought all the embassies were closed."

"There were only Syrian staff at the Canadian embassy, but the three of us had an interview with the actual Canadian consulate officer on Skype. Your mother, Naser, and I were sitting on this little couch, talking to this white man on the screen. He said he was in Lebanon. He even spoke some Arabic, son! You should've seen it! It was unbelievable!"

I wasn't sure what to say.

"So the man interviewed us. He was especially interested in whether or not I had ever served in Suddam Hussein's army when we lived in Iraq. Thank God, Bakr, I had that document that confirmed I paid my fee to the Iraqi government in order to bypass mandatory military service. Remember how I always tell you to have important documents on you, Bakr?"

Father rarely missed a chance for a life lesson. I pressed him further. "Sure, sure, *aiwa*, Father! And?"

"Well, at the end of that video call, he congratu-lated us, Bakr! He said, 'Welcome to Canada! We'll call you with details next week!'"

I gasped. "What?"

"Well, you can never be sure, so I didn't want to tell the rest of our family until it was certain. Bakr, we are moving to Canada!" He pronounced the word, *Canada*, so carefully.

My mind couldn't quite process it.

"*Bismillah*, we leave in a month . . . Abu Bakr?"

A beat of silence then I was screaming and jumping around as if I'd just won the World Cup. "Ahhhh! *Ya Allah!* Oh! My! God!" Father started laughing, tears in his eyes.

"Canada, Father? Really? This isn't one of your jokes, is it? This is real?"

He nodded, a grin lighting up his whole face, as he clapped me on the shoulder.

"*Ya Allah!* I can't wait to tell everyone!" I pulled my phone out.

He grabbed my phone. "Ai. Stop, Bakr. We cannot tell anyone except for family." Suddenly Father was serious. "We can tell Uncle Najim and Uncle Mohammed but no one else, okay? Do you understand why, Bakr?" I shook my head. "Kidnappings and ransom, Bakr. People are desperate. Don't forget we are living in a war. I've heard of people who are about to leave getting kidnapped. The kidnappers know the families will pay anything to escape. They'll squeeze anything they can get out of us. We have to be extra careful. No one but family, until we leave."

My brain slowly worked it out. "Wait . . . what do you mean we can only tell Uncle Najim and Uncle Mohammed? Aren't they coming too? We applied together."

Father sighed. "Sit, Bakr. There's more to tell you."

Together, we sat under the trees and Father slowly revealed the big secret. When we lived in Damascus, my uncles and Father received the amazing news that the United States had accepted our refugee application for the entire family. When they sat my mother, aunts, and Grandmother down to talk about it, Grandmother was adamant in her refusal. For years, she had lived under American occupation back in Iraq: "I will not live in America." For her, it was non-negotiable. Torn and anguished, Father had put his foot down, insisting that his children's safety was above everything else. Her only retort was, "You don't think it's dangerous for your family in America? There are other evils in this world, other than guns, Hafedh." Still, Father had accepted the offer while Uncle Najim and Uncle Mohammed turned it down. Uncle Mohammed didn't even bother to go to the security-screening interview with the UN; he simply skipped it. My mother was distraught, but what choice did she have? A few weeks after, it was all a moot point anyway because the United States suddenly suspended all refugee applications. Father's hopes for America slipped away. In the end, because of the increasing bombings in Damascus, he settled for moving back to Homs instead.

But now we were leaving. Leaving. We were going to a place without bombs and guns and I praised Allah with all my might. My heart soared with possibilities. I suddenly understood my father's tears. Something joyful felt like it was leaking, overflowing out of me. "When, Father? Next year?"

"November. We leave for Damascus next month. Everyone has to do a health screening. We'll meet our UN agent in Damascus and from there, he will give us what we need to fly to Canada." His eyes grew serious. "But Bakr, do you understand everything I'm trying to tell you? About Uncle Najim and Uncle Mohammed?"

"Sure, sure, Father. They didn't get their call yet but they'll be a few months behind us, right?"

"No, my son. Uncle Mohammed didn't even go to his interview. You know how stubborn he is and how devoted he was to Grandmother. He felt like going to the interview would be a betrayal of her wishes. So . . . no. They aren't leaving."

"Yousef? Aziz? They have to stay here?"

"Yes, son."

It was too much: I couldn't make sense of anything so I just stared at my sneakers.

"Bakr, I know this news isn't easy, but Uncle Najim's family shouldn't be too far away from their call. And, *bismillah*, Uncle Mohammed will get out of Syria some way or other. Who's stronger than Mohammed?" Father stood and clapped my back, "Come, son, we have much to do. We leave in a month."

Leaving. Canada. Those words flashed through my brain again and again. But, my cousins. Oh my God, what about my cousins? And what would I pack? Do they play soccer in Canada? Where exactly is Canada? I had never been on a plane before. Questions whirled about in my head as Father led me back home to tell my sisters the unbelievable news.

The next day, we had a big family lunch at our place with all my uncles and aunts and cousins. The apartment was bursting at the seams with twenty-four people, and we were a nervous ball of energy waiting for Father to break the news. It was a feeling somewhere between weighty dread and bursting excitement. Finally, Father's chair scraped on the floor as he stood and we all turned towards him.

"The UN called and we are moving to Canada next month," he said simply.

It was a mess of laughter, squeals, shouts, disbelief, and tears. Everyone was on their feet and talking at once. Aziz and Yousef had me in a tight huddle. Then they were jumping, hands over gaping mouths, slaps, high fives, bear hugs.

I faced an onslaught of questions from my cousins. Questions I didn't know the answers to or hadn't even had enough time to come up with myself. Finally, dizzy with emotion, I looked over at Father and he, Uncle Najim, and Uncle Mohammed were locked in a tight embrace, tears silently trickling down, the relief and love in the room completely palpable. Our family was happy for us, unreservedly.

14

NOVEMBER 2014

If God Allows It

Just as Father said, I waited until the last week before our departure to tell my friends. It wasn't easy. I felt so guilty. I was leaving my friends and family behind in this mess. I was going to safety, but where were they going?

I could barely stand the thought of leaving any of them behind, but our friends and family never once begrudged us our good luck. They told us how lucky we were, without a trace of jealousy.

Especially in that last week, I heard *inshallah* a lot. If God allows it. "We will be together again, *inshallah.*" "We will see each other soon, in Canada! *Inshallah!*" "We will find safety eventually, *inshallah.*"

As we frenetically tried to pack our entire lives into two bags each, I started giving away my things to my friends and cousins. One day, in front of that garden wall that was now a pile of rubble, I waited for Amro, just as I had a thousand times before. Staring down at my soccer ball, I remembered the day I got it more than three years ago. It was just after Father insisted on the nighttime curfew and, my God, I was late getting home. Amro, Aziz, Yousef, and I had been out trying new soccer tricks we had seen on YouTube. Aziz booted my brand new Adidas soccer ball, the one that Father bought me for my birthday, and it vanished. Amro thought the neon yellow ball had sailed over a tall stone wall with barbed wire coiled at the top. Yousef insisted it had rolled down an alley. We spent an hour searching the streets, and talked about sneaking into the courtyard, but the barbed wire scared us. I sulked all the way home, bracing myself for a marathon lecture about the new curfew and responsibility. The next morning, I was still stinging from the loss when those three showed up on my front step with a brand new ball they had pooled their money together to buy for me. Now, as I waited for Amro, I juggled that same soccer ball on the top of my right foot. The ball rolled off and I heard a familiar snort of laughter.

"Ha! I can still beat you, Bakr! W'Allah!" Amro's shouts bounced down the empty streets. He ran a few steps to catch the escaping ball.

"*Inchibb!* You'll need a decent ball to practise with if you're going to beat me." I nodded at the ball. "It's yours now."

Amro bent over to pick the ball up and cradled it in his hands. He gulped hard. "Thank you, my brother." Suddenly, we were in a fierce hug. Amro released me and clapped me on the shoulder. "*Inshallah.* There's always WhatsApp." We both smiled.

The day before we left Homs, I invited Yousef to our apartment, which was dotted with suitcases, bursting full. Dozens of boxes filled with random household items we wouldn't be taking with us: shampoo, mixing bowls, old towels. Draped in white sheets, our furniture looked like ghosts. Yousef burst in in his usual way then stopped abruptly, startled by the sight of our lives, all packed up.

"Yousef?"

He stared at my ratty soccer shoes sitting on the plastic mat next to the front door. He looked up at me and burst into tears. I couldn't find the right words. What do you tell your brother when you're leaving him behind? Wordlessly, we headed out into the little yard. The chickens were sold by then; only four budgies and two canaries remained.

I walked over to those cheerful cages alive with birdsong. I whistled and the birds replied as I opened the door to one of the cages. My favourite sky-blue budgie hopped out immediately and flitted to perch on my head, as usual. This never failed to make me smile.

"Yousef, I want you to take my birds."

He looked up at me, then up at my budgie nestled in my hair, and after a pause, nodded slowly. "It's really happening, isn't it? I still can't believe it. That month went too fast."

I inhaled deeply. "I know."

I knew we were both thinking about his father skipping that UN interview. Things were different then, back in Damascus. No one ever thought the violence would still be going on, especially not Grandmother. Neither of us dared talk about it, though. "It'll be okay. We'll find a way to bring you to Canada, too. *Inshallah*. I have faith. Brothers forever."

Yousef's eyes were brimming with love. "Brothers forever," he whispered.

For our final dinner in Homs, twenty-six of us were packed in our empty apartment: all of Uncle Mohammed's and Uncle Najim's family, plus two of Father's closest friends. Later that night, after my uncles, aunts, and girl cousins had returned to their homes, the boys hung around even though my whole family was exhausted. Friends had been dropping by all week to say their goodbyes and we felt drained of tears. My parents and sisters were doing last minute preparations inside the apartment.

The night was unusually warm, considering it was November. It was nearly pitch-black, except for some light from surrounding apartments. The streetlights on our street had been shot out long ago, but the stars were bright above us and the moon glowed. Yousef, Aziz, Abdullah, Ali, Naser, and I leaned against our crumbled garden wall, as we had done a thousand times before. We just talked, sharing stories, remembering stupid things, teasing each other, wondering about the future. Everyone took turns guessing what Canada would be like, how our lives would change there.

"*Ya Allah!* You're both gonna end up with Canadian girlfriends!" Aziz clapped his hands with glee and we doubled up in snorting laughter.

"Don't be stupid, Ziz!" I laughed at him.

"Aiiiii! Who's getting a blond girlfriend?"

That distinctive, whooping yell could only be Amro, strutting towards us with a bunch of other friends. He jumped and danced towards us and we all shouted greetings and shook hands. More jokes, more teasing, more old soccer stories.

"Hey, are you going to make Team Canada, Bakr?" Yousef teased.

Eventually, we all fell quiet with our own versions of what this fantasy of Canada could possibly be like. Softly, Aziz broke the silence. "You know what I wish? What I pray to Allah for? I want us *all*," he gestured at the whole circle, "to be safe in Canada. I don't care how cold it is. We'll freeze our butts off together. I want everything as it is . . . us, together, hanging out . . . but in Canada."

"Yeah," Amro chimed in. "And if we can't be together, then you can't forget us. Never forget us. Never forget Syria. Or Iraq, for that matter."

Everyone nodded in agreement. It seemed impossible to me, to forget them.

"Yeah, and don't forget Islam, it is your heart. And Bakr, do something good for Syria. Show them our suffering. Tell your story," Yousef said.

Tell my story? That seemed like an even crazier, far-fetched idea than forgetting my cousins and friends. How? It seemed like an impossibly big task. I turned towards Yousef. "*Inshallah*."

15

Damascus in a Different Light

Packing up the van on that November morning,
I couldn't help but think about our move from Iraq
four years ago, or even our move to Damascus just
last year. Except this time, it was only the ten of
us. A second van, jammed full with our twenty
pieces of luggage, followed behind. We were silent,
lost in our own thoughts. I sat in the back staring
out the window, watching the streets of Homs slip
by, possibly for the very last time. I tried hard to
memorize every last detail. The way the crowded

souk smelled, all the stalls selling vegetables, halal meat, fruit, tea, spices, and sweets. My mother's favourite store to buy scarves and fabric. I pretended to hate going there because it always took such a long time, but I secretly loved walking amongst all the bolts of vibrant silks and cottons and running my hands through this soft world. I never really realized how bright, crowded, and colourful my world was until I had to leave it.

Once we reached Damascus, the reality was really setting in. The vans dropped us off at a rundown hotel. Four other refugee families were arriving, overloaded with bags. As we all worked at unloading our luggage and getting to our hotel rooms, Father went to meet with the International Organization for Migration agent. He returned to our rooms clutching a thick white plastic bag with the dark blue IOM logo on it. I stared at that picture for a long time: a globe partially split in half, with a family holding hands in the middle. Our last name, al Rabeeah, was written on the front in thick black marker. Father clasped this bag as a fiercely protective mother does her newborn baby. Gathering us around him, he emphasized how important the bag was, how it must be with him at all times: it had all our documents and tickets, as well as instructions and contacts for emergencies. Father explained that we would fly in ten days. Before we left, Uncle Najim, Abdullah, Uncle Mohammed, and Aziz would join us to see us off. "In the meantime, buy whatever you think you need, but remember we only have two bags each. I don't know if we will return, so enjoy the city." He reminded us all that my mother and sisters could not go out unless he, Naser, or I was with them. "Documents all the time and watch for the *shabiha*. No mistakes now. We're very close."

Those ten days flew by faster than we ever expected them to. We spent hours wandering the rows of covered shopping arcades that Damascus was famous for, and even I had fun. I bought new clothes for my new life in Canada. What would I need? What would other kids look like? I bought three watches even though I had never worn a watch before. It just felt like a grown-up thing to have.

One of the best things about our time in Damascus was visiting Umayyad mosque. When we'd lived in Damascus for six months, we had not visited this magnificent place, but during those ten days, we went to Umayyad three times. It was unlike any mosque I had ever been to. It is one of the oldest and largest mosques in the world and it is sacred in Islam. The beauty of it stunned me.

We attended one Friday service there, and when I entered the wide inner sanctuary, all I could do was stare. The air was cool and hushed. The carpet was a deep, rich red. Majestic marble columns and elaborate arches soared above us and stretched luxuriously down the entire width of the building. The giant chandeliers looked like they dripped with sun-dipped jewels. Usually, the sanctuaries of mosques were plain spaces because we were supposed to focus on worship, but here, standing shoulder to shoulder with so many people, in this beautiful place, I couldn't help but think how lucky we were. As we went through the *Jum'ah* service, I felt blessed. I felt like God wanted me to remember the love of brotherhood, the love of community, and the rich beauty that surrounds us. Even though it was chilly in this great stone and marble building, my heart was warmed by the love I had for my religion, my God, my family, my country. I bowed in deep, reaching gratitude.

Outside in the sunny courtyard, people milled about on the marble floor, worn smooth from the centuries of feet that had explored it. I especially loved walking along the sides of the courtyard, craning my neck until it was sore, gazing at the gigantic mosaics. It was unbelievable how much detail was made by those tiny tiles. Giant palm and date trees, fantastic houses, flowing patterns. Some gleamed with silver and gold, but mostly there were a lot of blues and greens, which made me think of lush forests and deep lakes. It reminded me of a life full of living, growing things, not of dusty, bombed-out streets. I hoped, deep inside, Canada would bring green back into our lives.

All around me in this sacred place, little kids Abrar and Alush's age ran about playing games and screeching. Some boys kicked a soccer ball around. A group of women in hijabs and *abayas* ate their lunches from plastic bags. This felt like a true Muslim's life to me: real life soaked in the wonder of prayer and devotion.

THREE DAYS BEFORE OUR DEPARTURE, Uncle Najim, Abdullah, Uncle Mohammed, and Aziz joined us. In his rush to catch the Damascus bus, Aziz had missed breakfast. He was starving, so he and I went to a cafe. He inhaled four sandwiches and on his last bite, I stood up. "This one's on me, Ziz," I said as I pulled out my new wallet. Then I looked at the bill: 1500 lira. It was nearly double the price than it was at the start of the civil war but it was worth it, just to see the look on Aziz's face.

My cousin looked up at me in utter shock, his mouth still full. "What?" Aziz mumbled through a mouthful of bread and swallowed hard. "You've never treated before! Big man, now!" He laughed, slapped the table, nodded with approval, and smiled big at me. Pride? Was that the look in his eyes? He nodded again to himself and slapped me on the back. "Thank you, brother."

16

DECEMBER 12, 2014

The Last Squeeze

The morning of our departure was chaotic with everyone trying to move our luggage to the street, all the while dreading the last moment of goodbye. The other four families were doing exactly what we were trying to do — bring a lifetime of bags to wait on the curb using the hotel's one tiny, slow elevator. Finally, our twenty bags were brought down and we couldn't stall anymore. It was time.

Father reached for Uncle Najim and Uncle Mohammed. No words. Just tears. The three of them embraced for a long time, heads bent together, almost in prayer. Eyes closed tight. Our fathers' tears caused us all to cry. We couldn't help it. At last, I turned towards Abdullah and Aziz, their eyes already swimming. They both bent down slightly to me and when I felt our heads bump gently together, a wave of sadness hit me so hard, I was breathless. It was quiet, except for sniffing and the occasional choking sob. As we moved about, hug to hug, person to person, we tried hard to swallow the sadness but it stuck in our throats, in our chests. Uncle Najim held me by the shoulders to look at me for a few seconds then he pulled me close. "Soon," he managed, "we'll see you soon." I nodded because I believed it.

Uncle Mohammed. He enfolded me and his warm smell brought fresh tears. He smelled like home. I just stayed in his arms and wept because there was no holding that grief in. At least with Uncle Najim, we had "soon." With Uncle Mohammed, I had no idea what would happen. He released me. "Be good, Bakr. You will have such a big life in Canada. Goodbye."

Aziz wavered in front of me. The impossibility of saying goodbye ate us both. His bear hug. That's all we did: hugged.

Then, as raw as we felt, it was done. The business of departing took over: our uncles and cousins left in a taxi and Father disappeared into the hotel lobby to check out. We stood on the curb, eyes focused down the street. Standing a few steps away from my family and at the edge of the sidewalk, I leaned out to see if I could spot our bus in the busy street.

Out of nowhere, two SUVs veered in front of us. One stopped directly in front of me, nearly hitting me. The five families exchanged panicked looks. *Shabiha* spilled out of their cars, eyed everyone's bags, and started circling. We all looked down and my sisters huddled together. "Hey! You! Boy! Come!" Keeping my head bowed, I raised only my eyes, hoping the voice wasn't calling me. I met a man's cold glare. "Documents! Passports! What's going on here?" the man barked at me. I could see his gun. My mouth gaped open but no words came out. Something deep inside told me not to give him our passports. Where was Father? Naser was with Mother, and he held onto Alush. I looked at him and his eyes had no answers either.

"What are you, deaf? Documents! Passports!" A few other people started slowly rooting around their bags, stalling. I pretended to rustle through my backpack . . . but if they had our passports, what would stop them from keeping them? That familiar voice inside me again, "*run*," and my feet twitched in response. I looked up, alarmed.

Was there an alley nearby I could disappear into? Would I be fast en —

"*Stop!*" Father's voice boomed through my fear. "We are waiting for the UN!" His white plastic bag was brandished before him, both hands gripping the bag. The other four fathers were behind him, a parade of IOM bags. Those plastic bags were like a magical talisman. Those five fathers wielded them like triumphant banners high over their heads, faces set in grit and determination. The thugs shrunk back.

The man who yelled at me put his hands up in mock surrender and a big fake smile. "Just a routine document check! IDs, *please*," he snorted.

Ten minutes: that's how long it took them to check everyone's documents. I gripped my backpack the entire time. We had lived through shootings, raids, and massacres, and those ten minutes were the most horrifying ten minutes I had ever experienced. When the SUVs finally peeled away, I could breathe again.

Father chuckled and looked at me. "I think that was our last *shabiha* squeeze, son."

17

Buses, Airports, and Selfies

When the UN pulled up in front of the hotel, my heart leapt. It was one of the most exciting things I had ever seen. It wasn't just a little bus — it was a whole convoy. In front was a white SUV with UN in bold black lettering, and following it were two shiny black buses. At the back, another white UN SUV. Eight men in bright sky-blue vests. It all looked so official and safe. We had been on many buses before but somehow, this bus felt big.

The IOM agent, an Arabic woman wearing over-sized sunglasses, stepped out of one of the buses and welcomed us. She read off the five family names in a loud, clear voice. The fathers reached into their white bags and pulled out the necessary papers. The drivers opened up the exterior storage bins on the side of the bus and started loading up the luggage. Some of the men in the blue vests came out to help us. A scramble for bags and we loaded in: Mother and my sisters first, then the boys, with Naser practically running to get on, and Father last. You could tell he was mentally counting us off, no one left behind.

As we settled in, two by two, the IOM agent explained the three-hour ride to the international airport in Lebanon and the breaks we would take. The IOM agency would provide us food throughout the entire journey. At every airport, there would be someone who spoke Arabic to take us to where we needed to go and to get us our plane tickets. Her smile was warm, reassuring, confident. In my heart, I thanked God again.

That bus ride was a long one and we were sweltering in our new Canadian clothes. As I watched the mountains roll by, I just tried to see everything, remember everything. I felt scared. What was our life going to be like? What would school be like? Every time I'd imagined my new life, I thought I would just understand everything: that somehow by being there, the language would absorb into my skin. But as I searched my brain, the only English word I could remember was *thanks*. Were there mosques in Canada? Where would we live? Would Father find work? Would Naser? What about internet? And my phone? The questions came, wave after wave. I tried to close my eyes to them, to sleep, to pray, to recite my favourite parts of the Q'uran, to think about the best soccer games we ever played. Nothing, only this nervous knot inside me. I think we were all flooded with fears because we all started talking, as if to keep the questions at bay. Moving between our seats and chatting constantly, we recalled old stories, old memories. Remember when . . . remember when . . . remember when . . .

Finally, the airport. By now it was early evening and the sky was all pinks and deepening purples. A dark blue band grew in the sky. The airport in Lebanon was so big and people rushed around everywhere. The IOM agent deposited us in a waiting area. We were to stay there until three in the morning when a different agent would meet us, give us our tickets, and take us to our departure gate. We were given vouchers for dinner and we settled into our little makeshift camp. You could tell the day was particularly wearing on the adults because most of them stretched out on the benches to close their eyes. Father used our 10M bag as his pillow. Soon, even the kids settled down to sleep. Some my age had their earphones in, texting furiously away on their phones. Selfies. Everyone took selfie after selfie the whole day. Father especially.

For me, sleep was impossible. This time, it wasn't the questions. It was the people! I loved the humming sound of all those wheeled suitcases zipping by. There were so many different kinds of people. I saw my first Chinese woman. I saw a young guy with a bushy beard, just like many Muslim men had, but his was blond. I laughed. It was incredible and I loved it. Yes, of course I had seen lots of American movies and soccer games on TV but watching all these strangers walk right by me was exciting. In Syria and Iraq, you could look at a man and say, he is Saudi, she is Iranian, he is Lebanese. We could just tell because we looked slightly different, but these other differences were fascinating! Adventure and wonder bubbled up in me.

At last, another agent approached with an open smile. It was time to fly to Italy.

THE AIR ON THE AIRPLANE was strange:
it hummed. My throat felt dry and lights were
oddly bright. Lebanon to Rome. We shuffled and
squeezed by, confused about where our seats were.
We tried to jam our carry-on bags into those bins
above the seats but they were narrow and our
backpacks were bursting full. We plunked down
in the tiny seats, with me next to the window,
Aiesha, then Father in the aisle seat. Across the
aisle, Abeer laughed at Father, who tried to arrange
his long legs while peering out the tiny windows
at the orange lights of the runway and murmuring
"Inshallah" to himself. I looked at his hands gripping the tiny armrests and laughed. "Father! You're
okay! See? No problem!" I winked and grinned at
him. How many times had I heard him tease me
that way?

But I was terrified too. When I heard the
engines come to life, I pulled my seat belt even
tighter. A crackly voice spoke to us over the
speakers while the flight attendants pointed to
the little monitors in front of us that talked about
emergency procedures. Never before had I paid
so much attention to a video. Masks? Flotation
devices? Ya Allah. When the main cabin lights
flickered out, I was glad it was nighttime so I
couldn't see the ground out the window. Where

were the emergency exits again? The plane moved slowly, and then it stopped altogether. I was afraid everyone could hear my heart pounding in my throat. I snuck a peek at Aiesha to see her eyes squeezed shut, lips murmuring a quiet prayer. Father nodded once, reassuringly, at me.

Then, the plane roared to life and surged forward. The balls of my feet dug into the floor and I leaned far back into my seat as we raced faster and faster. The runway screamed below me, the gigantic metal wings caught the air, and the plane climbed up, up, up. *Ya Allah, ya Allah, ya Allah.* It wasn't so much a prayer as it was a plea.

18

DECEMBER 13, 2014

Enroute to Canada

We arrived in Rome. More waiting, another IOM agent, another flight, but this time to Toronto on an even bigger plane. The other four families had scattered on their own journeys to other foreign countries so we were alone. On the first plane, Father had been merely nervous, but the idea of spending ten hours in the air really scared him. He prayed a lot on the long flight and so did Naser, actually. Back in Syria, Naser had been lazy with his devotions at best, but on the plane, Naser was devout in his prayers. By this time, I had slept so little that I was too exhausted to pray with my family.

A few hours into the flight, Naser leaned forward in his seat. He had been watching a movie but he pulled his headphones out and looked like he was concentrating, really hard. I looked at my brother and pulled my headphones out.

"What are you doing, Naser?"

He continued to squint at the seat in front of him.

"Naser?"

"Shhh! I'm trying to listen!" He waved me away.

"Listen? To what?" I sat still. I didn't hear anything except the sounds of the plane.

"The people in front of us."

I listened again. "You mean the people speaking English? You don't understand English, stupid!" I scoffed at him. Naser was about as studious as I was.

"No, no! W'Allah, there are a few words I can make out."

I rolled my eyes at him. "Fine, genius. What are they saying then?"

"Inchibb," he waved me away again, "They're talking . . . about . . . fine, I don't know what they're saying . . . Bakr, do you think we'll ever understand what they are saying?" He turned to me with genuine worry in his eyes.

A snort from across the aisle. "Probably not!" Father laughed at us.

ONE MORE MOVIE LATER, the flight attendants started to tidy up the cabin and people rustled about. We peered out the windows and saw a fury of white. Naser jumped out of his seat and started rummaging in the overhead bin. He pulled out his bag and headed for the bathroom. Weird.

A few minutes later, the seat belt sign came on and the captain announced we were starting to descend. Naser came shuffling back with his jacket and a hat on. He looked different. Bizarre, somehow. I sat there, studying him as he shoved his backpack under the seat in front of him. He fastened his seatbelt and started loosening it. That's it: he looked fatter.

"Naser? Why . . . wait, did you put more clothes on?"

He looked at me, dead serious, as if trying to decide whether he should tell me something or not. Father leaned across the aisle to see what we were up to. Now, my sisters looked at him too. Naser turned to Father, then back to me.

"Did you see the snow out there?" he stuttered. "So I put all my clothes on, what's the big deal?"

Father practically spat and we laughed at Naser, all puffed up from the extra layers. He had on all his spare clothes from his bag. And that's how we landed in Toronto, laughing at my brother.

The plane finally stopped and we were in the aisle, gathering our bags and waiting to leave the plane, Naser peering out the window. Indeed, the whole world looked white, white, white. Snow whipped furiously about outside the plane.

"Oh my God. We are all going to die in the cold!" Naser leaned as far back away from the window as he could, shaking his head to himself the whole time.

Father grinned and clapped Naser on the back. "Snow? No problem!" He looked at me, eyes alight. "What is snow, but frozen rain? It's a good sign, right, Bakr?"

19

Edmonton

The final plane. When we had landed in Toronto, it was dark and snowing so we couldn't see much. Our flight to Edmonton was during the morning so I was able to see our new country. There was so much land. It stretched out in a canvas of whites, greys, and browns below us like a messy patchwork of prayer rugs, but it all looked empty, somehow.

By the time we landed in Edmonton, we were exhausted. Jet lag jumbled up our sleeping and eating and we had travelled so much in the last two days that we couldn't tell what time or day it was. We just wanted to settle in and stay in one place for a long time.

Inside the airport terminal in Edmonton, we were greeted by volunteers holding a big welcome sign with our name on it. I had no idea who these people were but my heart lifted at the sight of the neon sign and even brighter smiles. They helped us gather our luggage and a translator explained that we would be staying at an agency called the Reception House for the first ten days until we moved to our permanent home.

The people at the Reception House were kind. Translators explained what our new life in Edmonton would be like. We had a few English classes, lessons about the money, a tour of the neighbourhood. Constant paperwork to be filled out — every afternoon, there was something new for all the adults to sign. I think Canadians need a form for everything they do. Back in Syria, if you wanted something, you just paid money and did it. Here: forms, forms, forms. And though we were cramped in our tiny quarters at the Reception House, no one dared to venture out into the bitingly cold winter streets. My sisters, especially, were adamant about not leaving our space. It was all too intimidating to go out on our own. I didn't know these streets and I was afraid of getting lost.

After the first three days at the Reception House, we had to start buying our own food. Father returned with stories of visiting his very first Chinese grocery store. Even though he laughed about not being able to utter a word of English, I could tell he was flustered by the experience. We couldn't read the signs or ask for help. The money was colourful and confusing. This was especially difficult for Father, who was so used to taking care of everything. And though we sat and listened to the volunteer translators explaining everything, we weren't always able to entirely understand their Arabic dialects. Still, just listening to Arabic felt soothing and comforting. A little taste of home, like standing under a warm shower. I loved letting the rolling sounds wash over me.

Those first weeks were a grey blur and it was a relief to finally move to a space of our own, to stretch out and not feel like guests anymore. To flop down somewhere and start to think of something as our own.

We were lucky that Mother had a distant cousin in Edmonton already. Assad had come to Canada six years before and he helped us find our first home. That last day at the Reception House, we piled into three taxis with all our nineteen bags. Yes, nineteen. The airline lost one of our bags: mine.

Ya Allah. Gone were two of my brand new watches I never got to wear. Gone were some of my old favourite clothes. Gone were the gifts and mementos friends had given me before we left.

In the taxis, we stared as this strange new city rolled by. The brown, slushy streets with big trees strung up with little lights. Big supermarkets with parking lots jammed with cars. What was disconcerting was there were hardly any people walking in the streets. Our translator explained that it was Christmas Eve and that Christmas was a major holiday in Canada. Is this why there were no people in the street? I remember our big holiday, Ramadan, and the streets clogged with people shopping, visiting, and celebrating.

This was so very different from Syria and Iraq and my heart ached a little, the coldness of the air seeping into my stomach where sadness and nervousness paired together in a tumbling, rolling kind of feeling in my stomach.

Our taxis finally stopped in front of our new home. "Welcome!" chirped the translator. She waited out front with our tall, stern-looking landlord. As we gawked, my sisters squealed at the little houses around us with their peaked roofs. Individual family homes were rare in Homs, but back in Iraq, we'd lived in a large, sprawling house.

But Iraqi houses all had flat roofs and before now,
I had only ever seen those triangular roofs in
movies. Our new home was white with bright
red trim. Later, I would learn the word *duplex*,
but all I knew was that it was like two houses
glued together. I liked the idea that there was
another family living on the other side of our wall.
It seemed less lonely.

Suddenly everyone was talking all at once as
we pulled our bags out of the taxis. Inches of snow
covered the front yard and Alush jumped right
into it, playing and squealing. One by one, we
stepped inside and Father breathed in deeply as he
surveyed the main floor.

Then, the translator and landlord launched
into an endless talk. While Mother and my sisters
waited in the living room, Father, Naser, and I
followed the two from room to room. The landlord
talked about how to care for every single room, as
if we had never lived in a house before. He patted
the walls gingerly and reminded us to be very
careful with the walls. I knocked on the walls.
Yup, solid with a bit of a hollow sound. Surely they
wouldn't just fall down, but by the way our landlord kept going on about them, you'd think that
they would collapse any moment. After a tour
of all the rooms, we were finally alone as a family.

Father looked at us, then at Naser and I. He patted the walls gingerly, just like the landlord: "Yes, here we are in this lovely home, but be very, very careful with these Canadian walls!" His eyes twinkled with mischief and Father leaned right against the wall and gave it a loud, theatrical kiss. "See? Very careful! Very good Canadian walls!"

20

Back to School

All of us were going back to school, even Mother, Father, Maryam, Naser, and Abeer. The adults were going to English language classes every morning while Aiesha and Asmaa started high school, and I returned to junior high. Abrar and Alush were off to elementary. We joked about doing homework together around the kitchen table. All the women were exemplary students, and they were excited to begin their studies. The guys? We groaned a little on the inside. Studying had never really been our strong suit, but this was our new life so we were going to tackle it together.

The first Monday, Father, Naser, and I set out to tour our new schools. I was a nervous ball of excitement when we set out for Highlands, my new junior high. What would it be like? Would the teachers like me? Father and Naser listened to me rattle off questions and just as we turned the corner, we stopped and gawked. The building was beautiful. It was an old red brick building with soaring windows. Archways, stone-framed bay windows, a little bell tower. It didn't look at all like the flat, white, boxy schools we had in Syria.

"Surprise, Bakr! You're not going to school, you're going to court!" teased Father. He was right. The court building in Homs looked a little like this, old and grand. My heart gave a little high-kick.

At the front entrance, we met an Arabic translator from the Reception House. He led us through the school but the halls were mostly empty. As we walked past opened doors, I saw students already busy in their lessons. It made me feel oddly shy.

We were led to an office filled with art and pictures where a tall woman named Ms. Dobson met us and she explained, in a soft voice, that she was the assistant principal of Highlands Junior High. She had light blue eyes behind her purple glasses and her hair was long and blond. The translator, Naser, and Father sat down in her office while I stood, bolt-straight, arms folded, and tried to listen hard. There was a blur of information and after a while, all I could really do was stare at the paintings and photographs on the side of the filing cabinet directly in front of me. It wasn't that I didn't want to pay attention. I was very interested in everything that was going on, but I couldn't help but think that I had never once been in any school office before. In Syria and Iraq, all staff areas were forbidden to students. Here, students strolled in and out of the office.

I was relieved to hear that I wouldn't have to be in with all the students right away. My first few weeks would be spent learning English with a volunteer tutor in the library. This teacher, Ms. Maggie, came to the office and introduced herself. We went to the library together where we met another unusual sight: a dog. In the library, Ms. Dobson and our translator introduced another teacher, Ms. Mayer. My two new teachers beamed at us and I looked back and forth for a bit because they looked much the same to me but then something nudged my leg and I jumped back. I had forgotten about the big, white dog. Laughter and more English in soothing tones. I heard, "Okay?"

and then an expectant silence as the two teachers looked at me. I searched my brain for English but only one word came. "Thanks."

The translator rushed to translate but, already, I was flustered. Was this what it was going to be like for the rest of my life? My stomach hurt.

After the tour and meeting more teachers, I felt exhausted. My brain was too full. Father was pumped up with energy as he clapped his hands together and said brightly, "Great! When does Bakr start? Tomorrow?" Naser just laughed at me so I pulled myself a little taller. "Sure, sure, let's go."

THE NIGHT BEFORE my first actual day of school, I laid out my clothes for the big day in the room I shared with Naser and kept chattering about my new school. He could tell I was nervous so he let me talk but he just kept saying, "It's okay, Bakr. It will be fine." Finally, around, midnight, he turned the lights off and said, "Quit worrying. Go to sleep," and turned over in his bed. I lay there in the dark, staring up at the ceiling and trying hard to fall asleep but my mind kept racing. Finally, around two in the morning, he sat up, sighed, and snapped on his lamp. "Bakr. Stop. I can practically hear you thinking. Leave it to God. You will be fine. I know this."

Naser, my gruff brother, looked at me gently. In that moment, I saw his own loneliness, his own fears. His pain at having left his free, independent life and friends in Syria. I wondered whatever happened to that girl in the café. He knew the insecurities and heaviness in my heart because he carried them too. "Aiwa," I nodded. We exchanged half smiles and he turned off his lamp again. Feeling a little less alone, I slowly drifted into a fitful sleep.

The next morning as I shivered on my walk to school, I didn't pass a single person. A few cars drove by but no one walking. It reminded me of what the streets in Homs were like after the chaos and panic of a bombing or massacre, when everyone hid in their homes.

I arrived at the school and still, I saw no one. Where were all the students? I went in through the side door. Not a soul. Did I get the time wrong? I checked my watch. Oh. Almost a whole hour early. The halls were ghostly quiet. *Bismillah*, I prayed under my breath. Okay, library. I remembered being told to go there but I had no idea where the library was. I stamped the snow off my shoes and finally got up the courage to look around. I hoped I wouldn't see anyone because I didn't know what to say. I hoped I would see someone because I felt lost. My steps echoed too loudly. Then, I peered around a corner and my breath caught. Trees. A mosaic of soaring white trees set amongst dazzling purple, blue, green flourishes. Umayyad mosque. My heart leapt at the distant memory and my breathing evened out a little. I turned. More stairs, far down the way and another mosaic. A big glass case filled with art and other beautiful objects. Oh, maybe this was right. I kept walking down the hall and found the familiar library door. There, I sat on a blue bench and waited.

As the hallways slowly filled with the sounds of the school day starting, more and more students streamed by. Just like school in Syria, the students ran, shouted, and jostled each other as they walked past me. I was too afraid to make eye contact. All at once, everything seemed so loud. I hated this fear inside me. It felt stupid and childish and I was ashamed of it, but it was too overwhelming.

Finally, a soft voice said my name. I looked up and tried my best to smile. I could do this. This was my new life so I had to do this.

She gestured clearly to herself and said, "Ms. Maggie." She tugged gently on the dog's leash: "Rue." The dog yawned loudly and I laughed. Oh no, that brought on an onslaught of English. So me: "Thanks." She stood and gestured for me to follow her.

Ya Allah, another blitz of English as Ms. Maggie
opened the library door and flipped on the lights.
I couldn't understand a word but it felt rude
not to say anything so I kept repeating "Thanks."
I struggled to find any other word, number, name
of movies, but nothing. Only "Thanks." I blushed
furiously. Some gesturing. Sit? Okay, I could sit.
I tried hard to look up at her but couldn't. I didn't
want to be disrespectful or offend anyone but it
was just too much. I wanted to go home.

At that thought, I realized that I wanted
Syria because Homs was still home to me. In my
twenty-six days in Canada, I had not heard or seen
a single bomb or gun. There was no fighting, no
war. I was glad to be here, to be safe. Some kind
of impossible knot inside me had released but
now, I was just a different kind of afraid. I had
prayed so long for safety but now, I felt ungrateful
and ashamed and I couldn't help it. The backs of
my eyes started to sting and I clenched my teeth
because I didn't want to start my new life with
tears.

Ms. Maggie said something to me and patted
my arm. The dog nudged and snuffled at my hand
and I shrank back a little. Rue sighed loudly and
flopped down at my feet under the table. He put
his head on my foot and sighed again and I couldn't

help but smile. "Abu Bakr?" Ms. Maggie waved her phone at me and gestured at my backpack. Her fingers danced on her screen and she held her screen up to me. "Good morning, how are you?" in beautiful, beautiful Arabic words. I gasped.

"Google Translate." Ms. Maggie laughed and gave me a thumbs-up. She pointed at my bag again and at her phone so I handed my new phone to her and she pointed at the passcode. I punched the number in. "Google Translate," she repeated, and she showed me my phone. Oh! She was downloading a translation app for me. This felt instantly better.

And so my first morning at school passed slowly. Words, phrases, tentatively, hopefully, typed into our phones. Sometimes she gave me a confused look when I showed her the English translation. Sometimes I chuckled at the garbled Arabic that came through. Ms. Maggie taught me a few words and phrases. She showed me the alphabet. Desperately, I hoped my English classes in Syria would come rushing back but the only words I remembered were "Yes" and "No." Lunchtime came and Ms. Maggie urged me to go downstairs to the dining room to get something to eat. It was even halal. I was so surprised that they knew what halal was. Through her phone again, she explained that there were other Muslim students in the school and there would always be a halal or vegetarian option for lunch.

For the first time since we'd left Damascus, warmth seeped into me. It felt a bit like how I felt whenever I stood with all the people at mosque. To know that someone had thought to prepare halal food, that someone had taken my religion into account rather than ignore or be afraid of it, it felt like such a blessing. Before leaving Syria, everyone had warned me not to lose Islam — as if moving to a non-Muslim country would wipe out my faith — but here, people wanted to honour it.

Still, the idea of a hot lunch did not tempt me enough to want to leave the library. I could hear all the kids shouting and running outside in the halls and it seemed impossibly chaotic. All I really wanted was to be alone, so I shook my head. More questions, more gentle encouragement, but Ms. Maggie could see that I wasn't going to budge so she finally left me alone.

At last. After a morning of words, words, words, I was grateful for the quiet. I closed my eyes and soaked in the stillness. I didn't realize how noisy my life was back in Syria until we came to Canada. Here, it was so quiet. No rumbling explosions, rattling gunfire, or wailing sirens.

But also no boisterous crowds or rowdy gangs of cousins. I opened my eyes and looked around me. I was surrounded by shelves of books with colourful spines: some skinny, some thick, some serious-looking, others bright and fun. I wondered what stories those books held.

I flopped back down in my chair, boredom beginning to creep up on me. I checked my phone to see if Amro, Yousef, or Aziz had responded to my Facebook messages, but nothing. I wondered if my phone was working properly. Turning to face the tall windows, I stared at the twisting, graceful limbs of the bare trees. The sky, everything was washed-out January grey. I tried to imagine what spring would look like. These trees must be alive with green and this little bud of hope made me warm and sad all at once. My cousins. I glanced at my phone again, still no notifications. What were they doing right now? I passed the rest of that lunchtime lost in my memories.

On my second day of school, Ms. Maggie waved her cellphone at me. The Arabic words and her voice in English, "Do you want to go and see your prayer room?" Rue raised his head at "go." Even the dog knew more English at me. I nodded. Yesterday, in the whirlwind and nerves of my first day, I had totally forgotten to pray throughout the day.

This morning, I carefully put my prayer rug in my backpack but then I wondered if Muslim students prayed at school. During the meeting with Ms. Dobson and the translator, she had explained that they were trying to set up a prayer room for me, but I wondered if that meant no one else prayed at school.

I followed Ms. Maggie and Rue upstairs to the same hallway where my locker was. Again, the phone screen and Ms. Maggie asked, "Do you have a prayer rug?" I laughed. I loved that she knew what a prayer rug was. After another struggle with my lock, I had my prayer rug and she led me a few steps down the hall. She held the door open and more quick typing. "No one uses this space, except for the teachers who sometimes use the bathroom back there." I looked up from the screen and Ms. Maggie smiled, waving towards the back of the room. The screen flashed at me. "I'll be outside, waiting if you need me. Take your time."

With a whistle for Rue and the whoosh of the door closing, she was gone and I was alone. There were no lights on, but the window provided plenty of natural light. There were stacks of old chairs and a bulky desk. Trying to orient myself towards Mecca, I peered out the window. There was a small bathroom at the back of the room with a gleaming white sink and as the water ran, the sound of it took me back to all my mosques. I took extra care washing my hands, mouth, nostrils, face, head, and feet, then stepped back into the grey-carpeted room and turned to face the bathroom again. It felt odd to be standing in my school without my shoes and socks. I curled my toes under, self-consciously, then unfurled my prayer rug with a practiced flick of the wrist and kneeled on it.

As I went through the old, familiar prayers, something felt off. I paused and listened. What could it be? No bullets nor shattering glass. That was it: the stillness. No voices joined in prayer around me, no cousins having a fit of giggles. An old wooden desk to my right, a stack of plastic chairs to my left: that's all there was.

THAT FIRST WEEK went by in a mind-numbing, snail-paced daze. Time expanded and stretched in this disjointed way that seemed too slow to be real. One moment I was agonizing over the alphabet and the next moment, the week was done. My head constantly ached from straining to make myself understood. Even with the help of Google Translate, there were so many things I couldn't communicate. Every day after school, I trudged home and tried to sneak into my room without talking to anyone but, every day, Father peppered me with questions, dragging every reluctant word from me until I finally felt like myself again. Then, we would laugh at each other's halting new-found English.

Even though Father was doing his best to hold us together, we were each so wrapped up in our own kinds of loneliness that we got used to our little islands of grief. My sisters buried themselves in their books. With the help of Mother's cousin, Naser joined a gym and worked out for hours every day. Back in Homs in our cramped apartment, there were ten of us in three bedrooms. Living at such close quarters, we shared space and stories. Here in Edmonton, we were basically paired off into five much smaller bedrooms and with more doors, it was easy to close ourselves off. Talking about the darkness didn't bring any light, so we pushed it down in our own ways. It was a relief to be in a place free of the *shabiha* and snipers, but none of us had ever imagined the solitude we would face. We had traded the raucous, tearing war for a suffocating, quiet safety. No one could tell which was better, which was worse. It was both and neither.

21

A New Language

After the first few days, Ms. Mayer began spending more and more time with me. She was spirited and feisty. I joined her gym class. While Ms. Maggie was the serene tutor, Ms. Mayer was the bouncy teacher. Between my faltering English and mischievous Rue, Ms. Maggie was the ultimate example of patience. With everything — my English or even my math — she never once gave up on a lesson with me.

But Ms. Mayer, wow. We spoke the same language of sports. Ms. Mayer brought me in to play soccer many times and right away, I could tell she was a true athlete. She had incredible ball control and she could do tricks that I longed to learn. Maybe it was because she was an athlete and was used to reading opponents' body language in games, but she seemed to know when I was frustrated or upset. Even when I refused help, she knew that bringing me a soccer ball would help ease that knot inside me. She just let me deal with my turmoil in my own way, with a soccer ball.

One day, Ms. Maggie wasn't at school and I had to join the regular classes. I had no idea what was going on. All I knew was that I had to stay in the class with all these kids I didn't know. I guess that's not entirely fair. Over the weeks, many kids had come up to me at different points to say hi and tell me their names. Everyone smiled at me but then they carried on in their fast-talking world.

I sat in this classroom abuzz with conversation and I couldn't explain why this anger was welling up in me. I tried to breathe through it but I couldn't. I snapped the Chromebook screen shut and instantly felt bad about my little tantrum, but when I flipped it back open, I couldn't log back on.

I tried a few times, slowly punching in all the letters as carefully as possible. Nothing. The frustration welled up again. Why was everything so difficult? Back in Syria, everyone told us how lucky we were to have a chance at a good life in Canada. But when would this good life begin? When would it get easier? Better?

My chair scraped the floor loudly as I stood and approached the teacher, Mr. Gray. I liked him because he was also the soccer coach and he had joined Ms. Mayer and me a few times when we were just kicking a ball around. I showed him the piece of paper Ms. Maggie had written out for me, asking to go to the washroom. He smiled and nodded and I bolted out of the classroom.

In the quiet hall, I tried to remember which direction to go. *Ya Allah.* Where? I wandered for a bit, my father's joke bouncing around my buzzing brain. On the tour, he had teased me about not mixing up the girls' and boys' washrooms. I double-checked before entering the deserted washroom. As I ran the tap, the whoosh of the water soothed me a little. It made me think of *wudu.* I splashed my face and stared at myself hard in the mirror.

Back upstairs, I thought I heard Ms. Mayer's voice and I instantly felt better. She would understand. I wandered from classroom to classroom, trying to peek in to see if she was in one of the rooms, but I couldn't find her.

I was just outside Mr. Gray's room again and I just stood there, willing myself to go back in. My fingernails dug into my palms. How could I possibly be complaining? I knew I shouldn't feel like this; I knew how lucky we were to get out of that stupid civil war alive. I just wanted to feel safe. This was ridiculous to me because my brain knew I was safe. There were no MIGs flying overhead. No giant fireballs. No officer staring me down while he toyed with his rifle. How could I be so childish? I swallowed hard and squeezed my eyes shut. Amro and his cackling laugh. Aziz with his too-cool selfie faces. Yousef. His tears in my old apartment that last day. I could do this. I placed both my palms to my face and washed these memories over my eyes, over my head, down my neck, just like in *wudu*. Aiwa, let's go.

SOCCER. It was the beautiful game that finally made my heart settle in. After watching a few soccer matches and gym classes, I joined in with the other students. It felt wonderfully ordinary to be with a bunch of kids, kicking the ball around just for fun.

In mid-March, I was pulled onto the Grade Nine team to play the teachers in the final game of the lunchtime intramurals. The gym was filling with giddy, rambunctious students as they clambered onto the stage to watch the match. The students and teachers chirped back and forth at each other and I laughed at this unbelievable sight. I might not have understood the language but I knew that assured strut, that cocky upward tilt of the chin, the smug smiles and shouts. I loved it. It was Amro and Ali and my cousins all over again. I loved even more that the teachers dished it right back. I could never imagine my teachers back in Syria or Iraq doing any of this, never mind having fun with it.

The whistle blew and it was a rush of energy. It all came back. Drive, grit, looking, always looking. Cheers, shouts, jeers, so much laughing. I was hot, sweating, and out of breath. It felt fantastic. It didn't matter how little English I spoke but by then, I knew "pass," "goal," and "good game." Those words made me soar. In those words, I forgot the fear and I remembered who I really was. No bombs, no translators. Just me.

SEVEN MONTHS LATER a new school year begins — my last one at Highlands. I'm sitting in a different teacher's office in Highlands now. Her name is Ms. Yeung and her room is filled with paintings and photographs. There are weird, whimsical objects to look at and play with while we talk. A different dog — small, black, and playful Zoe — sleeps at my feet. Ms. Yeung is my Grade Nine English as a Second Language teacher. She tells me about the power of stories, and so we read books together and we trade tales about our families and our lives before Highlands. My English comes faster and easier as I discover words I need to use in order for her to understand. Sometimes, I need Google Translate, especially for the parts about the war, but mostly, I can grapple through the English.

One day, she starts our lesson with a question. "What is a secret wish you have?"

That's too easy. "To be a soccer player, Miss!"

She laughs, and says, "Okay, and what else?"

My last night with Amro, Yousef, Ali, Abdullah, and Aziz comes rushing back to me: my friends, the soccer games, the bombs, my cousins who are my brothers. How they told me to never forget.

I realize I carry Syria in my heart. I'm not sure if I'm ready to do this yet but I decide to trust and so, softly, I tell Ms. Yeung, "I want to share my story."

When I heard those words from Abu Bakr, they moved me deeply. I told him I wanted to write his story for him, as a gift. And that was how our story — Abu Bakr's and mine — started. I encouraged him to talk to his family first and two weeks later, he showed up in my office, fidgeting with a square of folded-up paper. "I'm ready, Miss, let's go."

We sat down and talked about how it may be difficult for him to recount everything. "Bakr, we stop this project anytime you want to, okay?"

He nodded. I had been teaching Bakr for two months and he was not usually shy with me, but he was now. "My family really likes the idea of you writing this. Actually, Miss, they can't believe it, that someone would want to hear about our lives. But, Father helped me make a list." Bakr unfolded the piece of paper, which revealed twenty-some items, written in Arabic.

I wondered how to begin. "Bakr, what is it like to live through a civil war?"

He patted his pockets, pulled out his iPhone, and began to type furiously. Google Translate. After a few moments, he turned his phone to me: "the escape from death is something so wondrous."

I was struck by the poetry of this awkward turn of phrase. Obviously, escaping death made a person feel gratitude, but *wonder*? In that moment, I fell in love with the project. Of course, it was filled with wonder because that word embodies gratitude, joy, and awe. Abu Bakr's infectious smile radiates these things. And so began months of after-school and lunch-time interviews. As our conversations deepened and my sketchbook filled with notes, questions, and pictures, we relied more on Google Translate. Although Bakr's English had progressed to the point where we could have basic conversations, the vocabulary he needed to describe a civil war was beyond him. For certain things like weaponry, he didn't even know the Arabic words, so we occasionally relied on image searches and charades to discover the vocabulary together. He showed me old cellphone photos and selfies; we looked up events he remembered on YouTube and news websites. Using Google Earth Street View, we explored the streets of Homs together and my heart leapt when I saw the yellow awning of Baserah Bakery. I researched the history and fact-checked key events; I read works of fiction and non-fiction because I wanted to try to understand Syria through the eyes of a journalist and an artist.

However, this isn't just Abu Bakr's story: it belongs to his family as well. I was able to interview the entire al Rabeeah family, first with translators, then without, as their English improved. This book started out as one boy's journey, but his parents' and siblings' perceptions and insights became equally important. Their recollections, our conversations, and my observations of them all became the palette I used to colour in the rough outlines Bakr and his list gave me. In that way, this book goes far beyond transcription or ghost-writing. I did my best to fully enter into their truth, to bring their stories to life at the level of the senses so that it could move others as much as it moved me. While I have relied on my imagination and research to fully enter their world and to make certain events more immediate, I have held to the facts as told to me by the family.

At the time of publication, Abeer, Aiesha, and Asmaa are contemplating post-secondary studies and like most young adults this age, their dreams shift from program to program. Abrar is now a student of mine, just like her cousin Raiyan was for one school year. Those girls brought their own sparkle to my writing. Alush is thriving in elementary school; the youngest truly do absorb the language with relative ease. Naser and Maryam have been able to find part-time employment, though it was not easy. As refugees, they are not allowed to hold a job without a work permit and the application process is a lengthy and difficult one. Hafedh struggles the most, being the patriarch who is relegated to English classes with his wife in the morning. My heart aches for Maryam and Naser; they are fairly close to my own age, so it is easy for me to imagine the full lives they left behind in Iraq and Syria. The isolation of being immigrants is difficult on all members of the family, but theirs must be a particularly wistful kind of loneliness.

Abu Bakr is grappling to find his place in this new life but he does so quietly. Teen angst spares no one and we laugh about how the universality of this truth is oddly reassuring. On occasion, he complains that Yousef and Aziz rarely reply to his messages and he fills me in on Amro's life in Germany. Amro, that boisterous, squawky teenager, endured a long, winding journey from Lebanon to Germany where he now contemplates job prospects and potential girlfriends, like any other young man.

Finally, the uncles, aunts, and cousins. Uncle Najim and his family arrived in Edmonton a year after Abu Bakr's family and they are flourishing here. After holding down the families' businesses as best he could, Uncle Mohammed and his family fled for Turkey. The refugee experience there is fraught with racism and instability, but at least they are safe from the bombs of Syria.

—WY, 2018

ENDNOTES

In writing this book, I drew on several texts to understand the broader context of the story of Bakr and his family. Reese Erlich's *Inside Syria: The Backstory of Their Civil War and What the World Can Expect* and Nikolaos van Dam's *The Struggle for Power in Syria: Politics and Society under Asad and the Ba'th Party* were invaluable.

Wherever possible, I cross-referenced specific events like shootings, bombings, and massacres with numerous internet resources and news reports such as Wikipedia, Human Rights Watch, Al Jeezera and other various Associated Press media outlets. Still, I must emphasize that this is not a journalistic work; it is based on one family's memories.

ABU BAKR'S ACKNOWLEDGMENTS

First, I want to thank Winnie for writing my story and my speeches. Thank you to Mr. Burns for supporting my dream. For all their love and help, I especially want to thank all the teachers and staff at Highlands Junior High.

I am grateful to Allah for blessing me with such amazing people in my life. Even with all the sadness and tragedy, I am thankful for all the love and life lessons I found along the way.

And, of course, thank you to my family for always being there for me. And, to my father, my best friend: thank you for showing me that laughter and joy are the true paths in life.

WINNIE'S ACKNOWLEDGMENTS

I will always be grateful to Abu Bakr and his entire family for being brave enough to share their story and, most importantly, for trusting me with it.

When we first came out with the self-published version of this work in June 2016, it was an exhilarating exercise in faith and fear that many people carried forward with their support and love. First, my gratitude to my biggest champion, Brad Burns. My self-published text was all the better because of the editing prowess of Andrea Hasenbank. And, to Karen Jacobsen who shaped that work and my person in meaningful ways. Jojo, your presence in my life gave me the courage to write and live authentically. *Thank you* is not enough.

For carrying this project to the next level, I am grateful to Kelsey Attard and Deborah Willis of Freehand Books for their gentle guidance and steadfast belief in me. And, for her savvy in shaping this diamond in the rough, I learned so much by working with Barbara Scott.

A very special thanks to the staff and teachers of Highlands Junior High: you do such amazing work with our students every day. To the countless Edmonton Public School Board consultants and teachers who rallied behind my work, I am so grateful. And, to my tribe of wise women, in particular Inie, Tanja, Sophia, and Angela, your friendship grounds me in all the different ways I need.

Finally, to my loud, crazy Chinese family, thank you for loving me exactly as I am. Mom, Dad, Sis: you have always allowed me to run free and chase after my dreams, but I always knew where home was because of you. Thank you.

ABU BAKR AL RABEEAH is currently a high school student. After three years of living in Canada, he enjoys his life here but he also dreams of a future where he can return to help rebuild Iraq and Syria.

WINNIE YEUNG has been an English Language Arts teacher for ten years. *Homes* is her first book. She lives in Edmonton, Canada, with her black pug, Zoe.